EASY RECIPES FOR THE
BREAD MACHINE

EASY RECIPES FOR THE
BREAD MACHINE

GET THE BEST OUT OF YOUR MACHINE WITH 50 IDEAS FOR ALL KINDS OF
LOAVES, SHOWN IN 250 STEP-BY-STEP PHOTOGRAPHS

JENNIE SHAPTER

southwater

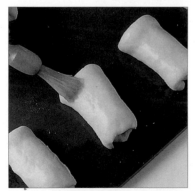

This edition is published by Southwater
an imprint of Anness Publishing Ltd,
Blaby Road, Wigston, Leicestershire LE18 4SE;
info@anness.com

www.southwaterbooks.com; www.annesspublishing.com

If you like the images in this book and would like to investigate
using them for publishing, promotions or advertising, please visit
our website www.practicalpictures.com for more information.

PUBLISHER: Joanna Lorenz
EDITORIAL DIRECTOR: Helen Sudell
EDITORS: Rebecca Clunes, Elizabeth Woodland and Kate Eddison
DESIGNER: Nigel Partridge
PHOTOGRAPHER AND STYLIST: Nicki Dowey and Toby Scott
HOME ECONOMIST: Jennie Shapter
PRODUCTION CONTROLLER: Wendy Lawson

© Anness Publishing Ltd 2013

A CIP catalogue record for this book is available from the British Library.

PUBLISHER'S NOTE
Although the advice and information in this book are believed to be accurate
and true at the time of going to press, neither the authors nor the publisher
can accept any legal responsibility or liability for any errors or omissions
that may have been made nor for any inaccuracies nor for any loss, harm
or injury that comes about from following instructions or advice in this book.

NOTES
Bracketed terms are intended for American readers.
American terms are only given in the list of ingredients for the small
size of bread machine: please refer to this ingredients list if you are making
bread in a larger machine.

The recipes in this book have all been written and tested for use in a
variety of bread machines available from leading manufacturers.
For best results, refer to your manufacturer's handbook to confirm
the proportion of flour to liquids. You may need to adjust the
recipes to suit your machine.

For all recipes, quantities are given in both metric and imperial measures and,
where appropriate, measures are also given in standard cups and spoons.
Follow one set, but not a mixture, because they are not interchangeable.
In particular, metric/imperial measures and cup conversions are not consistent
in order to accommodate the differences in absorption of different flours.

Standard spoon and cup measures are level.
1 tsp = 5ml, 1 tbsp = 15ml, 1 cup = 250ml/8fl oz.

Australian standard tablespoons are 20ml. Australian readers should use
3 tsp in place of 1 tbsp for measuring small quantities.

American pints are 16fl oz/2 cups. American readers should use
20fl oz/2.5 cups in place of 1 pint when measuring liquids.

Electric oven temperatures in this book are for conventional ovens.
When using a fan oven, the temperature will probably need to be reduced
by about 10–20°C/20–40°F. Since ovens vary, you should check with your
manufacturer's instruction book for guidance.

The nutritional analysis given for each recipe is calculated per loaf,
roll or item, unless otherwise stated. The analysis does not include optional
ingredients, such as salt added to taste.

Medium (US large) eggs are used unless otherwise stated.

Main front cover image shows Apple and Cider Seeded Bread – for recipe, see page 45

CONTENTS

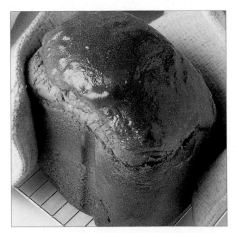

INTRODUCTION

The first automatic domestic bread-maker appeared on the market in Japan in the late 1980s, and since then bread machines have gained popularity all over the world. These excellent appliances have helped to rekindle the pleasure of making home-made bread, by streamlining the process and making it incredibly simple. All the "home baker" needs to do is to measure a few ingredients accurately, put them into the bread machine pan and push a button or two.

At first, it is easy to feel overwhelmed by all the settings on a bread machine. These are there to help you bake a wide range of breads, both sweet and savoury, using different grains and flavourings. In time, you'll understand them all, but there's no need to rush. Start by making a simple white loaf and watch while your machine transforms a few ingredients first into a silky, smooth dough and finally into a golden loaf of bread.

No matter what make of machine you have, it is important to focus on the bread, not the machine. Even the best type of

machine is only a kitchen aid. The machine will mix, knead and bake beautifully, but only after you have added the necessary ingredients and programmed it. Do not become frustrated if your first attempts do not look one hundred per cent perfect; they will probably still taste wonderful. There are a number of variables, including the type of ingredients used, the climate and the weather, which can affect the moisture level, regardless of the type of machine you are using.

The breads in this book are either made entirely by machine or the dough is made in the machine, then shaped by hand and baked in a conventional oven. Teabreads are mixed by hand and baked in the bread machine. Where the loaves are made automatically, you will usually find three separate lists of ingredients, each relating to a different size of machine. The small size is recommended for bread machines that are designed for loaves using 350–375g/12–13oz/3–3¼ cups of flour, the medium size for machines that make

ABOVE: Mix the dough for Pistolets in the machine and shape by hand.

loaves using 450–500g/1lb–1lb 2oz/4–4½ cups of flour and the large size for bread machines that are capable of making loaves using up to 600g/1lb 5oz/5¼ cups of flour. Refer to your manufacturer's handbook if you are not sure of the capacity of your machine.

It is very pleasurable to shape your own loaves of bread, and setting the machine to the "dough only" cycle takes all the hard work out of the initial mixing and kneading. The machine provides an ideal climate for the initial rising period, leaving you to bring all your artistry to bear on transforming the dough into rolls, shaped breads or yeast cakes. Once you master the technique, you can make breads from all around the world, including French Bread, American Breakfast Pancakes, Wholemeal English Muffins and Danish Pastries – to name but a few. It is also possible to make gluten-free breads, but as this is a specialist area, it is best to follow the instructions given by your manufacturer, or contact their helpline, if you wish to do this.

LEFT: To many people, a Farmhouse Loaf is the traditional bread they associate with their childhood.

GETTING DOWN TO BASICS

A bread machine is designed to take the hard work out of making bread. Like most kitchen appliances, it is a labour-saving device. It will mix the ingredients and knead the dough for you, and allows the bread to rise and bake at the correct time and temperature.

Bread machines offer a selection of programmes to suit different types of flour and varying levels of sugar and fat. You can explore making a whole variety of raw doughs for shaping sweet and savoury breads, sourdough breads, mixed-grains, Continental-style breads and many more.

All bread machines work on the same basic principle. Each contains a removable non stick bread pan, with a handle, into which a kneading blade is fitted. When inserted in the machine, the pan fits on to a central shaft, which rotates the blade. A lid closes over the bread pan so that the ingredients are contained within a controlled environment. The lid includes an air vent and may have a window, which can be useful for checking the progress of your bread. The machine is programmed by using the control panel.

LEFT: A typical bread machine. Although each machine will have a control panel with a different layout, most of the basic features are similar. More specialist cycles vary from machine to machine.

The size and shape of the bread is determined by the shape of the bread pan. There are two shapes currently available; one rectangular and the other square. The rectangular pan produces the more traditional shape, the actual size varying from one manufacturer to another. The square shape is mostly to be found in smaller machines and produces a tall loaf, which is similar to a traditional rectangular loaf that has been stood on its end. The vertical square loaf can be turned on its side for slicing, if preferred, in order to give smaller slices of bread.

BUYING A BREAD MACHINE

There is plenty of choice when it comes to selecting a bread machine to buy. Give some thought to which features would prove most useful to you, then shop around for the best buy available in your price range. First of all, consider the size of loaf you would like to bake, which will largely be governed by the number in your family. Remember that a large bread machine will often make smaller loaves but not vice versa.

You will need to consider whether the shape of the bread is important to you, and choose a machine with a square or rectangular bread pan accordingly.

Are you likely to want to make breads with added ingredients? If so, a raisin beep is useful. Does the machine have speciality flour cycles for wholemeal (whole-wheat) loaves? Would this matter to you? Another feature, the dough cycle, adds a great deal of flexibility, as it allows you to make hand-shaped breads. Extra features, such as jam-making and rice-cooking facilities, are very specialized and only you know whether you would find them worth having.

One important consideration is whether the manufacturer offers a well-written manual and an after-sales support system or help line. If these are available, any problems or queries you might have can be answered quickly, which is particularly useful if this is your first machine.

A bread machine takes up a fair amount of room, so think about where you will store it, and buy one that fits the available space. If the bread machine is to be left on the work surface and aesthetics are important to you, you'll need to buy a machine that will be in keeping with your existing appliances. Most bread machines are available in white or black, or in stainless steel.

Jot down the features important to you, listing them in order of your preference. Use a simple process of elimination to narrow your choice down to two or three machines, which will make the decision easier.

BUILT-IN SAFETY DEVICES

Most machines include a power failure override mode which can prove to be extremely useful. If the machine is inadvertently unplugged or there is a brief power cut the programme will continue as soon as the power is restored. The maximum time allowed for loss of power varies from 8 to 30 minutes, or more. Check the bread when the power comes back on; depending on what stage the programme had reached at the time of the power cut, the rising or baking time of the loaf may have been affected.

An over-load protection is fitted to some models. This will cut in if the kneading blade is restricted by hard dough and will stop the motor to protect it. It will automatically re-start after about 30 minutes, but it is important to rectify the problem dough first. Either start again or cut the dough into small pieces and return it to the bread pan with a little more liquid to soften the dough.

HOW TO USE YOUR BREAD MACHINE

The instructions that follow will help you to achieve a perfect loaf the first time you use your bread machine. The guidelines are general, that is they are applicable to any bread machine, and should be read in conjunction with the handbook provided for your specific machine. Make sure you use fresh, top quality ingredients; you can't expect good results with out-of-date flour or yeast.

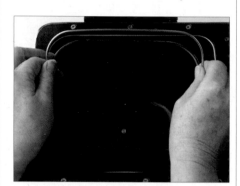

1 Stand the bread machine on a firm, level, heat-resistant surface. Place away from any heat source, such as a stove or direct sunlight, and also in a draught-free area, as these factors can affect the temperature inside the machine. Do not plug the bread machine into the power socket at this stage. Open the lid. Remove the bread pan by holding both sides of the handle and pulling upwards or twisting slightly, depending on the design of your particular model.

2 Make sure the kneading blade and shaft are free of any breadcrumbs. Fit the kneading blade on the shaft in the base of the bread pan. The blade will only fit in one position, as the hole in the blade and the outside of the shaft are D-shaped. Some machines are fixed blade only.

3 Pour the water, milk and/or other liquids into the bread pan, unless the instructions for your particular machine require you to add the dry ingredients first. If so, reverse the order in which you add the liquid and dry ingredients, putting the yeast in the bread pan first.

4 Sprinkle over the flour, ensuring that it covers the liquid completely. Add any other dry ingredients specified in the recipe, such as dried milk powder. Add the salt, sugar or honey and butter or oil, placing them in separate corners so they do not come into contact with each other.

EASY MEASURING

If you have a set of electronic scales with an add and weigh facility, then accurate measuring of ingredients is very easy. Stand the bread pan on the scale, pour in the liquid, then set the display to zero. Add the dry ingredients directly to the pan, each time zeroing the display. Finally, add the fat, salt, sweetener and yeast and place the bread pan in your machine.

5 Make a small indent in the centre of the flour (but not down as far as the liquid) with the tip of your finger and add the yeast. If your indent reached the liquid below the dry ingredients, then the yeast would become wet and would be activated too quickly. Wipe away any spillages from the outside of the bread pan.

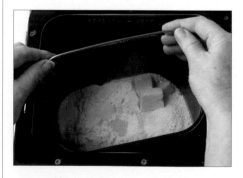

6 Place the pan inside the machine, fitting it firmly in place. Depending on the model of your machine, the pan may have a designated front and back, or clips on the outer edge which need to engage in the machine to hold the bread pan in position. Fold the handle down and close the lid. Plug into the socket and switch on the power.

7 Select the programme you require, followed by crust colour and size. Press Start.

8 Towards the end of the kneading process the machine will beep to alert you to add any additional ingredients. Open the lid, add the ingredients, and close the lid. If you have an automatic dispenser, add ingredients to this before starting the machine; it will add them at the correct time. Ingredients that may melt or stick should be added manually as described above. Check with your instructions.

9 At the end of the cycle, the machine will beep once more to let you know that either the dough is ready or the bread is cooked. Press Stop. Open the lid of the machine. If you are removing baked bread, remember to use oven gloves to lift out the bread pan, as it will be extremely hot. Avoid leaning over and looking into the bread machine when you open the lid, as the air escaping from the machine will be very hot and could cause you discomfort.

BELOW: A basic white bread is an excellent choice for the novice bread maker. If you follow these instructions and weigh the ingredients carefully, you are sure to achieve a delicious loaf of bread. Once you have gained confidence, try experimenting with the basic recipe, by adding other ingredients or changing the colour of the crust.

10 Still using oven gloves, turn the pan upside down and shake it several times to release the bread. If necessary, tap the base of the pan on a heatproof board.

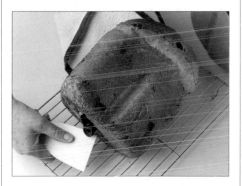

11 If the kneading blade for your bread machine is not of the fixed type, and comes out inside the bread, use a heat-resistant utensil to remove it, such as a wooden spatula. It will come out easily.

12 Place the bread on a wire rack to cool. Unplug the bread machine and leave to cool before using it again. A machine which is too hot will not make a successful loaf, and many will not operate if they are too hot for this reason. Refer to the manufacturer's manual for guidance. Wash the pan and kneading blade and wipe down the machine. All parts of the machine must be cool and dry before you store it.

BASIC CONTROLS

It will take you a little while and some practice to become familiar with and confident about using your new bread machine. Most manufacturers now produce excellent manuals, which are supplied with their machines. The manual is a good place to start, and should also be able to help you if you come up against a problem. Programmes obviously differ slightly from machine to machine, but an overview will give you a general idea of what is involved.

It is important to understand the function of each control on your bread machine before starting to make a loaf of bread. Each feature may vary slightly between different machines, but they all work in a basically similar manner.

START AND STOP BUTTONS

The Start button initiates the whole process. Press it after you have placed all the ingredients required for the bread-making procedure in the bread pan and after you have selected all the required settings, such as loaf type, size, crust colour and delay timer.

The Stop button may actually be the same control or a separate one. Press it to stop the programme, either during the programme, if you need to override it, or at the end to turn off the machine. This cancels the "keep warm" cycle at the end of baking.

TIME DISPLAY AND STATUS INDICATOR

A window displays the time remaining until the end of the programme selected. In some machines the selected programme is also shown. Some models use this same window or a separate set of lights to indicate what is happening inside the machine. It gives information on whether the machine is on time delay, kneading, resting, rising, baking or warming.

PROGRAMME INDICATORS OR MENU

Each bread machine has a number of programmes for different types of bread. Some models have more than others. This function allows you to choose the appropriate programme for your recipe and indicates which one you have selected. These programmes are discussed in more detail later.

PRE-HEAT CYCLE

Some machines start all programmes with a warming phase, either prior to mixing or during the kneading phase. This feature can prove useful on colder days or when you are using larger quantities of ingredients, such as milk, straight from the refrigerator, as you do not have to wait for them to come to room temperature before making the bread.

DELAY TIMER

This button allows you to pre-set the bread machine to switch on automatically at a specified time. So, for example, you can have freshly baked bread for breakfast or when you return from work. The timer should not be used for dough that contains perishable ingredients such as fresh dairy products or meats, which deteriorate in a warm environment.

CRUST COLOUR CONTROL

The majority of bread machines have a default medium crust setting. If, however, you prefer a paler crust or the appearance of a high-bake loaf, most machines will give you the option of a lighter or darker crust. Breads high in sugar, or that contain eggs or cheese, may colour too much on a medium setting, so a lighter option may be preferable for these.

WARMING INDICATOR

When the bread has finished baking, it is best to remove it from the machine immediately. If for any reason this is not possible, the warming facility will switch on as soon as the bread is baked, to help prevent condensation of the steam, which otherwise would result in a soggy loaf. Most machines continue in this mode for an hour, some giving an audible reminder every few minutes to remove the bread.

LEFT: French Bread can be baked in the machine on a French bread setting, or the dough can be removed to make the traditional shape by hand.

INTERIOR LIGHT

This button can be pressed to switch on a light within the machine. It lets you see clearly what is happening inside the machine through the viewing window and avoids opening the lid. The light will automatically switch off after 60 seconds.

LOAF SIZE

You have the option of making two or three sizes of loaf on most machines. Options vary according to the selected programme. The actual sizes vary between machines but approximate to small, medium and large loaves that range from around 500g/1lb 2oz to 1kg/2lb 4oz in weight. Some machines have medium, large and extra large settings, but the extra large is still smaller than the 1kg or 2lb loaf made by large machines. Check with the manufacturer's instructions for recommended quantities for each loaf size and then choose the closest setting.

BAKING PROGRAMMES

All machines have a selection of programmes to help ensure you produce the perfect loaf of bread. The lengths of kneading, rising and baking times are varied to suit the different flours and to determine the texture of the finished loaf.

WHITE OR BASIC

This mode is the most commonly used programme, ideal for white loaves and mixed grain loaves where white bread flour is the main ingredient.

RAPID

This cycle reduces the time to make a standard loaf of bread by about 1 hour and is handy when speed is the main criterion. The finished loaf may not rise as much as one made on the basic programme and may therefore be a little more dense.

WHOLE WHEAT

This is a longer cycle than the basic one, to allow time for the slower rising action of doughs containing a high percentage

ABOVE: Sun-dried tomatoes can be added to the dough at the raisin beep to make deliciously flavoured bread.

of strong wholemeal (whole-wheat) flour. Some machines also have a multigrain mode for breads made with cereals and grains such as Granary and rye, although it is possible to make satisfactory breads using either this or the basic mode, depending on the percentages of the flours.

FRENCH

This programme is best suited for low-fat and low-sugar breads, and it produces loaves with an open texture and crispier crust. More time within the cycle is devoted to rising, and in some bread machines the loaf is baked at a slightly higher temperature.

SWEET BREAD

A few bread machines offer this feature in addition to crust colour control. It is useful if you intend to bake breads with a high fat or sugar content which tend to colour too much.

CAKE

This setting can be used to mix and bake cakes. Most machines require a dry mix and a liquid mix to be added to the bread pan. The machine will then mix and bake. If your machine does not have this facility, teabreads and non-yeast cakes

can be easily mixed in a bowl and then baked in the bread pan on the bake or bake only cycle.

BAKE

This setting allows you to use the bread machine as an oven, either to bake cakes and ready-prepared dough from the supermarket or to extend the standard baking time if you prefer your bread to be particularly well done.

GLUTEN-FREE

A programme designed for gluten-free flour bread recipes and mixes.

RYE

A feature offered on one machine for making rye and spelt flour breads. Includes a kneading blade especially suited to kneading these doughs.

RAISIN BEEP

Some machines have an automatic dispenser, which can be filled with the extra ingredients before commencing the programme.

DOUGH PROGRAMMES

Most machines include a dough programme: some models have dough programmes with extra features.

DOUGH

This programme allows you to make dough without machine-baking it, which is essential for all hand-shaped breads. The machine mixes, kneads and proves the dough, ready for shaping, final proving and baking in a conventional oven. If you wish to make different shaped loaves or rolls, buns and pastries, you will find this facility invaluable.

OTHER DOUGH PROGRAMMES

Some machines include cycles for making different types of dough, such as a rapid dough mode for pizzas and Focaccia or a longer mode for wholemeal dough and bagel dough. Some "dough only" cycles also include the raisin beep facility.

Baking, Cooling and Storing

A bread machine should always bake a perfect loaf of bread, but it is important to remember that it is just a machine and cannot think for itself. It is essential that you measure the ingredients carefully and add them to the bread pan in the order specified by the manufacturer of your machine. Ingredients should be at room temperature, so take them out of the refrigerator in good time, unless your machine has a pre-heat cycle.

Check the dough during the kneading cycles; if your machine does not have a window, open the lid and look into the bread pan. The dough should be slightly tacky to the touch. If it is very soft add a little more flour; if the dough feels very firm and dry add a little more liquid. It is also worth checking the dough towards the end of the rising period. On particularly warm days your bread may rise too high. If this happens it may rise over the bread pan and begin to travel down the outside during the first few minutes of baking. If your bread looks ready for baking before the baking cycle is due to begin, you have two options. You can either override and cancel the programme, then re-programme using a bake or bake only cycle, or you can try pricking the top of the loaf with a cocktail stick to deflate it slightly and let the programme continue.

Different machines will give different browning levels using the same recipe. Check when you try a new recipe and make a note to select a lighter or darker setting next time if necessary.

Below: Use a cocktail stick to prick dough that has risen too high.

Removing the Bread from the Pan

Once the bread is baked it is best removed from the bread pan immediately. Turn the bread pan upside down, holding it with oven gloves or a thick protective cloth – it will be very hot – and shake it several times to release the bread. If removing the bread is difficult, rap the corner of the bread pan on a wooden board several times or try turning the base of the shaft underneath the base of the bread pan. Don't try to free the bread by using a knife or similar metal object, or you will scratch the non-stick coating.

If the kneading blade remains inside the loaf, you should use a heat-resistant plastic or wooden implement to prise it out. The metal blade and the bread will be too hot to use your fingers.

Above: Multigrain Bread is made with honey which, like other sweeteners, acts as a preservative. The loaf should stay moist for longer.

Below: Use a serrated bread knife when slicing bread so that you do not damage the texture of the crumb.

TO SERVE BREAD WARM

Wrap the bread in foil and place in an oven preheated to 180°C/350°F/Gas 4 for 10–15 minutes, to heat through. This is also a method that can be used to freshen bread.

COOLING

Place the bread on a wire rack to allow the steam to escape and leave it for at least 30 minutes before slicing. Always slice bread using a serrated knife to avoid damaging the crumb structure.

STORING

Cool the bread, then wrap it in foil or place it in a plastic bag and seal it, to preserve the freshness. If your bread has a crisp crust, this will soften on storage, so until it is sliced it is best left uncovered. After cutting, put the loaf in a large paper bag, but try to use it fairly quickly, as bread starts to dry out as soon as it is cut. Breads containing eggs tend to dry out even more quickly, while those made with honey or added fats stay moist for longer.

BELOW: Parker House Rolls can be frozen after baking, as soon as they are cool. They taste delicious warm, so refresh them in the oven just before serving.

ABOVE: If you are freezing bread to be used for toasting, slice the loaf first.

Ideally, freshly baked bread should be consumed within 2–3 days. Avoid storing bread in the refrigerator as this causes it to go stale more quickly.

Freeze cooked breads if you need to keep them for longer. Place the loaf or rolls in a freezer bag, seal and freeze for up to 3 months. If you intend to use the bread for toast or sandwiches, it is easier

ABOVE: Store bread with a crispy crust in a large paper bag.

to slice it before freezing, so you can remove only the number of slices you need. Thaw the bread at room temperature, still in its freezer bag.

With some loaves, however, freezing may not be a sensible option. For example, very crusty bread, such as French Couronne, tends to come apart after it has been frozen and thawed.

STORING BREAD DOUGHS

If it is not convenient to bake bread dough immediately you can store it in an oiled bowl covered with clear film (plastic wrap), or seal it in a plastic bag. Dough can be stored in the refrigerator for up to 2 days if it contains butter, milk or eggs and up to 4 days if no perishable ingredients are included.

Keep an eye on the dough and knock it back (punch it down) occasionally. When you are ready to use the dough, bring it back to room temperature, then shape, prove and bake it in the normal way.

You can make dough in your machine, shape it, then keep it in the refrigerator overnight, ready for baking conventionally next morning for breakfast. Cover with oiled clear film as usual.

Bread dough can be frozen in a freezer-proof bag for up to 1 month. When you are ready to use it, thaw the dough overnight in the refrigerator or at room temperature for 2–3 hours. Once the dough has thawed, place it in a warm place to rise, but bear in mind that it will take longer to rise than freshly made dough.

ABOVE: Store dough in the refrigerator in an oiled bowl covered in clear film or in a plastic bag.

ABOVE: Prepare rolls the night before and store in the refrigerator, ready to bake the following morning.

HAND-SHAPED LOAVES

One of the most useful features a bread machine can have is the dough setting. Use this, and the machine will automatically mix the ingredients, and will then knead and rest the dough before providing the ideal conditions for it to rise for the first time. The whole cycle, from mixing through to rising, takes around 1¾ hours, but remember it will vary slightly between machines.

KNOCKING BACK

1 At the end of the cycle, the dough will have almost doubled in bulk and will be ready for shaping. Remove the bread pan from the machine.

2 Lightly flour a work surface. Gently remove the dough from the bread pan and place it on the floured surface. Knock back (punch down) or deflate the dough to relieve the tension in the gluten and expel some of the carbon dioxide.

3 Knead the dough lightly for 1–2 minutes; shape into a tight ball. At this stage, a recipe may suggest you cover the dough with oiled clear film (plastic wrap) or an upturned bowl and leave it to rest for a few minutes. This allows the gluten to relax so dough will be easier to handle.

SHAPING

Techniques to shape dough vary, depending on the finished form of the bread you wish to make. The following steps illustrate how to form basic bread, roll and yeast pastry shapes.

BAGUETTE

1 To shape a baguette or French stick, flatten the dough into a rectangle about 2.5cm/1in thick, either using the palms of your hands or a rolling pin.

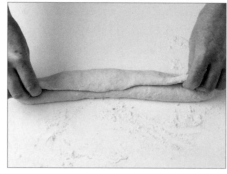

2 From one long side fold one-third of the dough down and then fold over the remaining third of dough and press gently to secure. Repeat twice more, resting the dough in between folds to avoid tearing.

3 Gently stretch the dough and roll it backwards and forwards with your hands to make a breadstick of even thickness and the required length.

4 Place the baguette dough between a folded floured dishtowel, or in a banneton, and leave in a warm place to prove. The dishtowel or banneton will help the baguette to keep the correct shape as it rises.

BLOOMER

1 Roll the dough out to a rectangle 2.5cm/1in thick. Roll up from one long side and place it, seam side up, on a floured baking sheet. Cover and leave to rest for 15 minutes.

2 Turn the loaf over and place on another floured baking sheet. Using your fingertips, tuck the sides and ends of the dough under. Cover; leave to finish rising.

TIN LOAF

Roll the dough out to a rectangle the length of the bread tin (pan) and three times as wide. Fold the dough widthways, bringing the top third down and the bottom third up. Press the dough down well, turn it over and place it in the tin.

COTTAGE LOAF

1 To shape a cottage loaf, divide the dough into two pieces, approximately one-third and two-thirds in size. Shape each piece of dough into a plump round ball and place on lightly floured baking sheets. Cover with inverted bowls and leave to rise for 30 minutes, or until 50 per cent larger

2 Flatten the top of the large loaf. Using a sharp knife, cut a cross about 4cm/1½in across in the centre. Brush the area lightly with water and place the small round on top.

3 Using one or two fingers or the floured handle of a wooden spoon, press the centre of the top round, penetrating into the middle of the dough beneath.

TWIST

1 To shape bread for a twist, divide the dough into two equal pieces. Using the palms of your hands, roll each piece of dough on a lightly floured surface into a long rope, about 4–5cm/1½–2in thick. Make both ropes the same length.

2 Place the two ropes side by side. Starting from the centre, twist one rope over the other. Continue in the same way until you reach the end, then pinch the ends together and tuck the join underneath. Turn the dough around and repeat the process with the other end, twisting the dough in the same direction as the first.

BREADSTICK

To shape a breadstick, roll the dough to a rectangle about 1cm/½in thick, and cut out strips that are about 7.5cm/3in long and 2cm/¾in wide. Using the palm of your hand, gently roll each strip into a long thin rope.

It may help to lift each rope and pull it very gently to stretch it. If you are still finding it difficult to stretch the dough, leave it to rest for a few minutes and then try again.

COURONNE

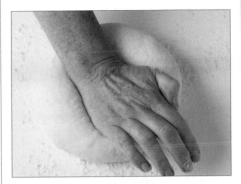

1 Shape the dough into a ball. Using the heal of your hand make a hole in the centre. Gradually enlarge the centre, turning the dough to make a circle, with a 13cm–15cm/5–6in cavity.

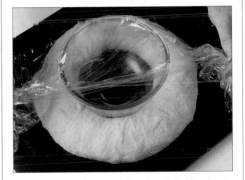

2 Place on a lightly oiled baking sheet. Put a small, lightly oiled bowl in the centre of the ring to prevent the dough from filling in the centre during rising.

SCROLL

Roll out the dough using the palms of your hands, until it forms a rope, about 25cm/10in long, with tapered ends. Form into a loose "S" shape, then curl the ends in to make a scroll. Leave a small space to allow for the final proving.

CROISSANT

1 To shape a croissant, roll out the dough on a lightly floured surface and then cut it into strips that are about 15cm/6in wide.

2 Cut each strip along its length into triangles with 15cm/6in bases and 18cm/7in sides.

3 Place with the pointed end towards you and the 15cm/6in base at the top; gently pull each corner of the base to stretch it slightly.

4 Roll up the dough with one hand from the base while pulling, finishing with the dough point underneath. Finally, curve the corners around in the direction of the pointed end to make the curved croissant shape.

BRAIDED ROLL

1 To shape a braided roll, place the dough on a lightly floured surface and roll out. Divide the dough into balls, the number depending on the amount of dough and how many rolls you would like to make.

2 Divide each ball of dough into three equal pieces. Using your hands, roll into long, thin ropes of equal length and place them side by side.

3 Pinch one of the ends together and plait the pieces of dough. Finally, pinch the remaining ends together and then tuck the join under.

FILLED BRAID

1 Place the dough for the braid on a lightly floured surface. Roll out and shape into a rectangle. Using a sharp knife, make diagonal cuts down each of the long sides of the dough, about 2cm/⅔in wide. Place the filling in the centre of the uncut strip.

2 Fold in the end strip of dough, then fold over alternate strips of dough to form a braid over the filling. Tuck in the final end to seal the braid.

PROVING

After the dough has been shaped, it will need to be left to rise again. This is sometimes referred to as proving the dough. Most doughs are left in a warm place until they just about double in bulk. How long this takes will vary – depending on the ambient temperature and richness of the dough – but somewhere between 30 and 60 minutes is usual.

Avoid leaving dough to rise for too long (over-proving) or it may collapse in the oven or when it is slashed before baking. Equally, you need to leave it to rise sufficiently, or the finished loaf will be heavy.

To test if the dough is ready to bake, press it lightly with your fingertip; it should feel springy, not firm. The indentation made by your finger should slowly fill and spring back.

ABOVE: A dough that has been shaped and placed in a bread tin to rise. The unproved dough should reach just over halfway up the tin.

ABOVE: Leave the dough in a warm, draught-free place to rise. This should take between 30 and 60 minutes. Once risen, the dough will have almost doubled in bulk.

SLASHING

Slashing bread dough before baking serves a useful purpose as well as adding a decorative finish, as found on the tops of traditional loaf shapes such as bloomers and French sticks. When the dough goes into the oven it has one final rise, known as "oven spring", so the cuts or slashes allow the bread to expand without tearing or cracking the sides.

The earlier you slash the dough the wider the splits will be. Depth is important, too: the deeper the slashes the more the bread will open during baking. Most recipes suggest slashing just before glazing and baking. If you think a bread has slightly over-proved keep the slashes fairly shallow and gentle to avoid the possibility of the dough collapsing.

Use a sharp knife or scalpel blade to make a clean cut. Move smoothly and swiftly to avoid tearing the dough. Scissors can also be used to make an easy decorative finish to rolls or breads.

SLASHING A SPLIT TIN OR FARMHOUSE LOAF

A long slash, about 1cm/½in deep, can be made along the top of the dough just before baking. You can use this slashing procedure for both machine and hand-shaped loaves. Using a very sharp knife, plunge into one end of the dough and pull the blade smoothly along the entire length, but make sure you do not drag the dough.

If flouring the top of the loaf, sprinkle with flour before slashing.

SLASHING A BAGUETTE

To slash a baguette, cut long slashes of equal length and depth four or five times along its length. A razor-sharp blade is the best tool for slashing breads. Used with care, a scalpel is perfectly safe and has the advantage that the blades can be changed to ensure you always have a sharp edge.

USING SCISSORS TO SLASH ROLLS

Rolls can be given quick and interesting finishes using a pair of sharp-pointed scissors. You could experiment with all sorts of ideas. Try the following to start you off.

• Just before baking cut across the top of the dough first in one direction then the other to make a cross.
• Make six horizontal or vertical cuts equally spaced around the sides of the rolls. Leave for 5 minutes before baking.
• Cut through the rolls in four or five places from the edge almost to the centre, just before baking.

ABOVE: Top rolls: making a cross; middle rolls: horizontal cuts around the side; bottom rolls; cuts from the edge almost to the centre.

BAKING BREAD WITH A CRISP CRUST

For a crisper crust, it is necessary to introduce steam into the oven. The moisture initially softens the dough, so that it can rise, resulting in a crispier crust. Moisture also improves the crust colour by encouraging caramelization of the natural sugars in the dough. Standing the loaf on a baking stone or unglazed terracotta tiles also helps to produce a crisp crust, the effect being similar to when breads are cooked in a clay or brick oven. The porous tiles or stone hold heat and draw moisture from the bread base while it is baking.

1 About 30 minutes before you intend to bake, place the baking stone on the bottom shelf of the oven, then preheat the oven. Alternatively line the oven shelf with unglazed terracotta tiles, leaving air space all around to allow for the free circulation of the hot air.

2 When ready to bake, using a peel (baker's shovel), place the bread directly on the tiles or baking stone.

3 Using a water spray bottle, mist the oven walls two or three times during the first 5–10 minutes of baking. Open the oven door as little as possible, spray the oven walls and quickly close the door to avoid unnecessary heat loss. Remember not to spray the oven light, fan or heating elements.

GLAZES

Both machine-baked breads and hand-shaped loaves benefit from a glaze to give that final finishing touch. Glazes may be used before baking, or during the early stages of baking to give a more golden crust or to change the texture of the crust. This is particularly noticeable with hand-shaped breads but good results may also be obtained with machine-baked loaves. Glazes may also be applied after baking to give flavour and a glossy finish. Another important role for glazes is to act as an adhesive, to help any topping applied to the loaf stick to the surface of the dough.

For machine-baked breads, the glaze should either be brushed on to the loaf just before the baking cycle commences, or within 10 minutes of the start of the baking cycle. Apply the glaze quickly, so there is minimal heat loss while the bread machine lid is open. Avoid brushing the edges of the loaf with a sticky glaze as this might make the bread stick to the pan.

Glazes using egg, milk and salted water can also be brushed over freshly cooked loaves. Brush the glaze over as soon as the baking cycle finishes, then leave the bread inside the machine for 3–4 minutes, to allow the glaze to dry to a shine. Then remove the loaf from the machine and pan in the usual way. This method is useful if you want to sprinkle over a topping.

For hand-shaped loaves, you can brush with glaze before or after baking, and some recipes, such as Parker House Rolls will suggest that you do both.

GLAZES USED BEFORE OR DURING BAKING

For a crust with an attractive glossy shine, apply a glaze before or during baking.

MILK

Brush on loaves, such as potato breads, where a softer golden crust is desired. Milk is also used for bridge rolls, buns (such as teacakes) and flatbreads where a soft crust is desirable. It can also be used on baps and soft morning rolls before dusting with flour.

OLIVE OIL

This is mainly used with Continental-style breads, such as Focaccia, Stromboli and Fougasse. It adds flavour and a shiny finish; and the darker the oil the fuller the flavour, so use extra virgin olive oil for a really deep taste. Olive oil can be used before and/or after baking.

BELOW: French Fougasse is brushed with olive oil just before baking.

BUTTER

Rolls and buns are brushed with melted butter before baking to add colour, while also keeping the dough soft. American Parker House Rolls are brushed before and after baking, while Bubble Corn Bread is drizzled with melted butter before being baked. Butter adds a rich flavour to the breads glazed with it.

SALTED WATER

Mix 10ml/2 tsp salt with 30ml/2 tbsp water and brush over the dough immediately before baking. This gives a crisp baked crust with a slight sheen.

EGG WHITE

Use 1 egg white mixed with 15ml/1 tbsp water for a lighter golden, slightly shiny crust. This is often a better alternative to egg yolk for savoury breads.

EGG YOLK

Mix 1 egg yolk with 15ml/1 tbsp milk or water. This classic glaze, also known as egg wash, is used to give a very golden, shiny crust. For sweet buns, breads and yeast cakes add 15ml/1 tbsp caster (superfine) sugar, for extra colour and flavour.

GLAZES ADDED AFTER BAKING

Some glazes are used after baking, often on sweet breads, cakes and pastries. These glazes generally give a glossy and/or sticky finish, and also help to keep the bread or cake moist. They are suited to both machine and hand-shaped breads.

BUTTER

Breads such as Italian Panettone and stollen are brushed with melted butter after baking to soften the crust. Clarified butter is also sometimes used as a glaze to soften flatbreads such as Naan.

HONEY, MALT, MOLASSES AND GOLDEN SYRUP

Liquid sweeteners can be warmed and brushed over breads, rolls, teabreads and cakes to give a soft, sweet, sticky crust. Honey is a traditional glaze and provides a lovely flavour, for example. Both malt and molasses have quite a strong flavour, so use these sparingly, matching them to compatible breads such as fruit loaves and cakes. Or you could mix them with a milder-flavoured liquid sweetener, such as golden (light corn) syrup, to reduce their impact slightly.

SUGAR GLAZE

Dissolve 30–45ml/2–3 tbsp granulated sugar in the same amount of milk or water. Bring to the boil then simmer for 1–2 minutes, until syrupy. Brush over fruit loaves or buns for a glossy sheen. For extra flavour, use rose water.

SYRUPS

Yeast cakes, such as Savarin, are often drizzled with sugar syrup, flavoured with liqueurs, spirits or lemon juice. The syrup moistens the bread, while adding a decorative topping at the same time.

PRESERVES

Jam or marmalade can be melted with a little liquid. Choose water, liqueur, spirits (such as rum or brandy) or fruit juice, depending on the bread to be glazed. The liquid thins the preserve and adds flavour. It can be brushed over freshly baked warm teabreads, Danish Pastries and sweet breads to a give a glossy, sticky finish. Dried fruit and nuts can then be sprinkled on top.

Select a flavoured jam to complement your bread or teacake. If in doubt, use apricot jam.

ICING SUGAR GLAZE

Mix 30–45ml/2–3 tbsp icing (confectioners') sugar with 15ml/1 tbsp fruit juice, milk, single (light) cream (flavoured with natural vanilla essence/extract) or water and drizzle or brush over warm sweet breads, cakes and pastries. You can also add a pinch of spice to the icing sugar to bring out the flavour of the loaf.

LEFT: The glossy top to Hot Cross Buns is achieved by glazing after baking with a mixture of milk and sugar.

TOPPINGS

In addition to glazes, extra ingredients can be sprinkled over breads to give the finished loaf further interest. Toppings can alter the appearance, flavour and texture of the bread, so are an important part of any recipe. They also allow you to add your own individual stamp to a bread by using a topping of your own invention.

MACHINE-BAKED BREADS

A topping can be added at various stages: at the beginning of the baking cycle, about 10 minutes after baking begins, or immediately after baking while the bread is still hot. If you choose to add the topping at the beginning of baking, only open the lid for the shortest possible time, so heat loss is limited to the minimum. Before you add a topping, brush the bread with a glaze. This will ensure that the topping sticks to the loaf. Most machine breads are brushed with an egg, milk or water glaze.

If applying a topping to a bread after baking, remove the bread pan carefully from the machine and close the lid to retain the heat. Using oven gloves, quickly loosen the bread from the pan, then put it back in the pan again (this will make the

ABOVE: Flaked almonds have been sprinkled over the top of this Raspberry and Almond Teabread, giving a broad hint of its delicious flavour and adding extra crunch.

final removal easier) then brush the loaf with the glaze and sprinkle over the chosen topping. Return the bread in the pan to the bread machine for 3–4 minutes, which allows the glaze to bake on and secure the topping. With this method, the chosen topping will not cook and brown in the same way it would were it added at the beginning of baking.

When using grain as a topping, the general rule is to match it to the grain or flour used in the bread itself; for example, a bread containing millet flakes or millet seeds is often sprinkled with millet flour.

If a flavouring has been incorporated into the dough, you may be able to top the loaf with the same ingredient, to provide a hint of what is inside. Try sprinkling a little grated Parmesan on to a cheese loaf about 10 minutes after baking begins, or, for a loaf flavoured with herbs, add an appropriate dried herb as a topping immediately after baking.

LEFT: Rolled oats and wheat grain are sprinkled on to Sweet Potato Bread just before it begins to bake to give the loaf a delightful rustic look.

FLOUR

To create a farmhouse-style finish, brush the loaf with water or milk glaze within 10 minutes of the start of baking and dust lightly with flour. Use white flour, or wholemeal (whole-wheat) or Granary (whole-wheat) for a more rustic finish.

CORN MEAL OR POLENTA

Use corn meal, polenta, semolina or other speciality flours as a finish for breads containing these flours, such as Courgette Country Grain Bread.

ROLLED OATS

These make a decorative finish for white breads and breads flavoured with oatmeal. Rolled oats are best added just before or at the very beginning of baking.

SMALL SEEDS

Seeds can be used to add flavour and texture in addition to a decorative finish. Try sesame, poppy, aniseed, caraway or cumin seeds. If adding sesame seeds immediately after baking, lightly toast until golden before adding.

LARGE SEEDS

Gently press pumpkin or sunflower seeds on to the top of a freshly glazed loaf to give an attractive finish and a bonus crunch.

PEPPER AND PAPRIKA

Freshly ground black pepper and paprika both add spiciness to savoury breads. This tasty topping can be added before, during or after baking.

SALT

Brush the top of a white loaf with water or egg glaze and sprinkle with a coarse sea salt, to give an attractive and crunchy topping. Sea salt is best applied at the beginning of baking or 10 minutes into the baking cycle.

WHEAT AND RYE FLAKES

These add both texture and fibre to bread as well as visual appeal. Sprinkle them over the top of the loaf after glazing at the beginning of baking.

ICING SUGAR

Dust cooked sweet breads, teabreads or cakes with icing (confectioners') sugar after baking for a finished look. If you like, add 2.5ml/½tsp spice before sprinkling.

HAND-SHAPED BREAD

All of the toppings used on machine-baked breads can also be added to breads that are hand-shaped and baked in an oven. There are several methods that can be used for adding a topping to hand-shaped rolls and breads.

SPRINKLING WITH FLOUR

If you are using flour, this should be sprinkled over the dough immediately after shaping and again before slashing and baking, to give a rustic finish. Match the flour to the type of bread being made. Unbleached white bread flour is ideal for giving soft rolls and breads a fine finish. Use corn meal, ground rice or rice flour for crumpets and muffins, and brown, wholemeal and Granary (whole-wheat) flours on wholegrain breads.

GROUND RICE OR RICE FLOUR

Muffins are enhanced with a ground rice or rice flour topping.

WHOLEMEAL FLOUR

Wholemeal (whole-wheat) flour toppings complement wholegrain dough whether made into loaves or rolls.

ABOVE: An Easter Tea Ring is glazed with an icing made from icing sugar and orange juice, then sprinkled with pecan nuts and candied orange.

ROLLING DOUGH IN SEEDS

Sprinkle seeds, salt or any other fine topping on a work surface, then roll the shaped but unproved dough in the chosen topping until it is evenly coated. This is ideal for coating wholegrain breads with pumpkin seeds or wheat flakes. After rolling, place the dough on the sheet for its final rising.

SESAME SEEDS

Dough sticks can be rolled in small seeds for a delicious crunchy topping.

ADDING A TOPPING AFTER A GLAZE

Some toppings are sprinkled over the bread after glazing and immediately before baking. In addition to the toppings suggested for machine-baked breads, these toppings can be used:

CANDIED FRUITS

Candied fruits make an attractive topping for festive breads and buns. Add the fruits after an egg glaze. Candied fruits can also be used after baking, with a jam or icing (confectioners') sugar glaze to stick the fruits to the bread.

NUTS

Just before baking, brush sweet or savoury breads and rolls with glaze and sprinkle with chopped or flaked (sliced) almonds, chopped cashews, chopped or whole walnuts or pecan nuts.

MILLET GRAIN, BLACK ONION SEEDS AND MUSTARD SEEDS

These small grains and seeds all add texture and taste to breads. Try them as a topping for loaves and flatbreads such as Lavash and Naan.

VEGETABLES

Brush savoury breads and rolls with an egg glaze or olive oil and then sprinkle with finely chopped raw onion, raw (bell) peppers, sun-dried tomatoes or olives for an extremely tasty crust.

CHEESE

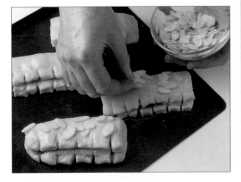

Grated cheeses, such as Parmesan, Cheddar or Pecorino, are best for sprinkling on to dough just before baking, resulting in a chewy, flavoursome crust.

FRESH HERBS

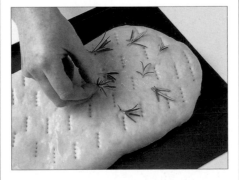

Use fresh herbs, such as rosemary, thyme, sage or basil for Italian-style flatbreads. Chopped herbs also make a good topping for rolls.

USING SUGAR AS A TOPPING

Sugar is available in many forms, so choose one appropriate for your topping.

DEMERARA SUGAR

Before baking, brush buns and cakes with butter or milk, then sprinkle with demerara (raw) sugar for a crunchy finish.

SUGAR COATING

Yeast doughs that are deep-fried, such as Doughnuts and Saffron Braids can be sprinkled or tossed in a sugar coating. Toss doughnuts in caster (superfine) sugar which has been mixed with a little ground cinnamon or grated nutmeg, or flavoured using a vanilla pod (bean).

DUSTING WITH ICING SUGAR

Use a fine sieve to sprinkle cooked buns and yeast cakes, such as Devonshire Splits and Calas, with icing sugar. Large cakes and breads such as Panettone, Kugelhopf and Strudel also benefit from a light dusting of icing sugar, as do fruit-filled Savarins. If serving a bread or cake warm, dust with icing sugar when ready to serve to avoid the topping soaking into the bread.

GETTING THE BEST FROM YOUR MACHINE

Even the most comprehensive bread-machine manual cannot possibly cover all the hints and tips you will need. As you gain experience and confidence you will be able to solve more and more of any little problems that crop up. Here are a few pointers to help you along the road to successful baking.

TEMPERATURE AND HUMIDITY

The bread machine is not a sealed environment, and temperature and humidity can affect the finished results. On dry days, dry ingredients contain less water and on humid days they hold more.

The temperature of the ingredients is a very important factor in determining the success of machine-baked bread. Some machines specify that all ingredients should be at room temperature; others state that ingredients can be added from the refrigerators. Some machines have preheating cycles to bring the ingredients to an optimum temperature of around 20–25°C/68–77°F, before mixing starts. It is recommended that you use ingredients at room temperature. Water can be used straight from the cold tap. Lukewarm water may be beneficial for the rapid bake cycle on cold days.

Hot weather can mean that doughs will rise faster, so on very hot days start with chilled ingredients, using milk or eggs straight from the refrigerator.

Icy winter weather and cold draughts will inhibit the action of the yeast, so either move your machine to a warmer spot, or warm liquids before adding them to the bread pan. On very cold days, let the water stand at room temperature for about half an hour before adding the other ingredients to the pan, or add a little warm water to bring it up to a temperature of around 20°C/68°F, but no hotter.

QUALITY PRODUCE

Use only really fresh, good quality ingredients. The bread machine can not improve poor quality produce. Make sure the yeast is within its use-by date. Yeast beyond its expiry date will produce poor results.

MEASURING INGREDIENTS

Measure both the liquids and the dry ingredients carefully. Most problems occur when ingredients are inaccurately measured, when one ingredient is forgotten or when the same ingredient is added twice. Do not mix imperial and metric measurements, as they are not interchangeable; stick to one set for the whole recipe.

Do not exceed the quantities of flour and liquid recommended for your machine. Mixing the extra ingredients may overload the motor and if you have too much dough it is likely to rise over the top of the pan.

FOLLOW THE INSTRUCTIONS

Always add the ingredients in the order suggested by the manufacturer. Whatever the order, keep the yeast dry and separate from any liquids added to the bread pan.

ADDING INGREDIENTS

Cut butter into pieces, especially if it is fairly firm, and/or when larger amounts than usual are required in the recipe. If a recipe requires ingredients such as cooked vegetables or fruit or toasted nuts to be added, leave them to cool to room temperature before adding them.

USING THE DELAY TIMER

Perishable ingredients such as eggs, fresh milk, cheese, meat, fruit and vegetables may deteriorate, especially in warm conditions, and could present a health risk. They should be only be used in breads that are made immediately. Only use the delay timer for bread doughs that contain non-perishable ingredients.

CLEANING YOUR MACHINE

Unplug the machine before starting to clean it. Wipe down the outside regularly using a mild washing-up liquid (detergent) and a damp, soft cloth. Avoid all abrasive cleansers and materials, even those that are designated for use on non-stick items, and do not use alcohol-based cleansers.

BREAD PAN AND KNEADING BLADE

Clean the bread pan and blade after each use. These parts should not be washed in the dishwasher as this might affect the non-stick surface and damage the packing around the shaft. Avoid immersing the bread pan in water. If you have difficulty extracting the blade from the pan, fill the base of the pan with lukewarm water and leave it to soak for a few minutes. Remove the blade and wipe it with a damp cloth. Wash the bread pan with mild washing-up liquid. Rinse thoroughly. Always store the bread machine with the kneading blade removed from the shaft. The bread machine and components must be dry before putting away. Some pans have a fixed blade.

ABOVE: A Granary loaf should be baked on the whole wheat setting, which has a longer rising cycle.

SPECIAL CONSIDERATIONS

Breads made with whole grains and heavier flours such as wholemeal (wholewheat), oatmeal or rye, or with added ingredients such as dried fruits and nuts, are likely to rise more slowly than basic white loaves and will be less tall. The same applies to breads with a lot of fat or egg. Breads that include cheese, eggs or a high proportion of fats and/or sugar are more susceptible to burning. To avoid over-cooked crusts, select a light bake crust setting.

WATCHING THE DOUGH

Keep a flexible rubber spatula next to the machine and, if necessary, scrape down the sides of the pan after 5–10 minutes of the initial mixing cycle. The kneading blade sometimes fails to pick up a thick or sticky dough from the corners of the pan.

COOLING THE BREAD

It is best to remove the loaf from the pan as soon as the baking cycle finishes, or it may become slightly damp, even with a "stay warm" programme.

CHECKING THE DOUGH

Check the dough within the first 5 minutes of mixing, especially when you are trying a recipe for the first time. If the dough seems too wet and, instead of forming a ball, sticks to the sides of the pan, add a little flour, a spoonful at a time. However, the bread machine requires a dough that is slightly wetter than if you were mixing it by hand. If the dough is crumbly and won't form a ball, add liquid, one spoonful at a time. You will soon get used to the sound of the motor and notice if it is labouring due to a stiff mix. It is also worth checking the dough just before baking, to make sure it isn't about to rise over the top of the bread machine pan.

ABOVE: Dough is too wet and requires more flour.

ABOVE: Dough is too dry and requires more water.

ADAPTING RECIPES FOR USE IN A BREAD MACHINE

After you have cooked a number of the recipes from this book you may wish to branch out and adapt some of your own favourites. This sample recipe is used to explain some of the factors you will need to take into consideration.

INGREDIENTS
Read the list of ingredients carefully before you start, and adjust if necessary.

MALT EXTRACT AND GOLDEN SYRUP
High sugar levels and/or dried fruit may cause the bread to over-brown. Reduce the malt extract and golden (light corn) syrup quantities by one-third and increase other liquids to compensate. Machine breads require the inclusion of sugar. Allow 5–10ml/1–2 tsp per 225g/8oz/2 cups flour.

BUTTER
High fat levels mean that the bread will take longer to rise. Reduce to 50g/2oz/ ¼ cup per 450g/1lb/4 cups flour. You may need to add an extra 30ml/2 tbsp liquid.

FLOUR
This recipe uses white flour, but remember that a wholemeal (whole-wheat) loaf works better if you replace half the wholemeal flour with strong white flour.

YEAST
Replace fresh yeast with easy bake (rapid-rise) dried yeast. In a wholemeal bread, for example, start by using 5ml/1 tsp for up to 375g/13oz/3¼ cups flour or 7.5ml/ 1½ tsp for up to 600g/1lb 5oz/5¼ cups flour.

MILK
Use skimmed milk at room temperature where possible. If you wish to use the time delay cycle you should replace with fresh milk with milk powder.

DRIED FRUIT
Additions that enrich the dough, such as dried fruits, nuts, seeds and wholegrains, make the dough heavier, and the bread will not rise as well. Limit them to about a quarter of the total flour quantity.

MALTED FRUIT LOAF
50g/2oz/scant ¼ cup malt extract
30ml/2 tbsp golden (light corn) syrup
75g/3oz/6 tbsp butter
450g/1lb/4 cups unbleached white bread flour
5ml/1 tsp mixed (apple pie) spice
20g/¾oz fresh yeast
150ml/5fl oz/⅔ cup lukewarm milk
50g/2oz/¼ cup currants
50g/2oz/⅓ cup sultanas (golden raisins)
50g/2oz/¼ cup ready-to-eat dried apricots
25g/1oz/2 tbsp mixed chopped (candied) peel
30ml/2 tbsp milk
30ml/2 tbsp caster (superfine) sugar

MAKES 2 LOAVES

1 Grease two 450g/1lb loaf tins (pans).
2 Melt the malt extract, syrup and butter in a pan. Leave to cool.
3 Sift the flour and spice into a large bowl; make a central well. Cream the yeast with a little of the milk; blend in the rest. Add the yeast mixture with the malt extract to the flour and make a dough.
4 Knead on a floured surface until smooth and elastic, about 10 minutes. Place in an oiled bowl; cover with oiled clear film (plastic wrap). Leave in a warm place for 1½–2 hours, until doubled in bulk.
5 Turn the dough out on to a lightly floured surface and knock back (punch down).
6 Gently knead in the dried fruits.
7 Divide the dough in half; shape into two loaves. Place in the tins and cover with oiled clear film. Leave to rise for 1–1½ hours or until the dough reaches the top of the tins.
8 Meanwhile, preheat the oven to 200°C/400°F/Gas 6. Bake the loaves for 35–40 minutes, or until golden. When cooked, transfer to a wire rack.
9 Gently heat the milk and sugar for the glaze in a pan. Brush the warm loaves with the glaze.

METHOD
Use a similar bread machine recipe as a guide for adapting a conventional recipe.

STEP 1
Obviously, you can only make one machine-baked loaf at a time. Make 1 large loaf or reduce the quantity of ingredients if your machine is small.

STEP 2
There is no need to melt the ingredients before you add them, but remember to chop the butter into fairly small pieces.

STEP 3
When adding ingredients to the bread pan, pour in the liquid first then sprinkle over the flour, followed by the mixed spice. (Add the liquid first unless your machine requires dry ingredients to be placed in the bread pan first.)

Add easy bake dried yeast to a small indent in the flour, but make sure it does not touch the liquid underneath.

Place salt and butter in separate corners of the pan. If your recipe calls for egg, add this with the water or other liquid.

Use water straight from the tap and other liquids at room temperature.

STEPS 4–8
Ignore these steps, apart from step 6. The bread machine will automatically mix, rise and cook the dough. Use a light setting for the crust due to the sugar, fat and fruit content of the Malted Fruit Loaf. Ordinary breads, such as a white loaf, need a medium setting; loaves that contain wholemeal flour should be baked on the whole wheat setting.

If you are adding extra ingredients, such as dried fruit, set the bread machine on raisin setting and add the ingredients when it beeps. If you do not have this facility, add approximately 5 minutes before the end of the kneading cycle.

STEP 9
Make the glaze as usual and brush over the loaf at the end of the baking cycle.

USEFUL GUIDELINES

Here are a few guidelines that are worth following when adapting your own favourite recipes.

• Make sure the quantities will work in your machine. If you have a small bread machine it may be necessary to reduce them. Use the flour and water quantities in recipes in the book as a guide, or refer back to your manufacturer's handbook.

• It is important that you keep the flour and the liquid in the correct proportions, even if reducing the quantities means that you end up with some odd amounts. You can be more flexible with spices and flavourings such as fruit and nuts, as exact quantities are not so crucial.

• Monitor the recipe closely the first time you make it and jot down any ideas you have for improvements next time.

• Check the consistency of the dough when the machine starts mixing. You may need to add one or two extra spoonfuls of water, as breads baked in a machine

ABOVE: Some conventional recipes call for you to knead ingredients, such as fried onions, into a dough. When adapting for a bread machine, add to the dough at the raisin beep.

require a slightly softer dough, which is wet enough to relax back into the shape of the bread pan.

• If a dough mixes perfectly in your machine but then fails to bake properly, or if you want bread of a special shape, use the dough cycle on your machine, then shape by hand before baking in a conventional oven.

• Look through bread machine recipes and locate something that is similar. This will give you some idea as to quantities, and which programme you should use. Be prepared to make more adjustments after testing your recipe for the first time.

BELOW: Use a similar bread machine recipe to help you adapt a bread you usually make conventionally. For example, if you have a favourite swede bread recipe, try adapting a machine recipe for parsnip bread.

USING BREAD MIXES

Packaged bread mixes can be used in your machine. Check your handbook, as some manufacturers may recommend specific brands.

• Check that your machine can handle the amount of dough the bread mix makes. If the packet quantity is only marginally more than you usually make, use the dough cycle and then bake the bread conventionally.

• Select an appropriate setting; for instance, use the white/basic or rapid/fastbake setting for white bread.

1 Place the recommended amount of water in the bread pan.

2 Spoon over the bread mix and place the pan in the machine.

3 Select the programme required and press Start. Check the consistency of the dough after 5 minutes, adding a little more water if the mixture seems too dry.

4 At the end of the baking cycle, remove the cooked bread from the bread pan and turn out on to a wire rack to cool.

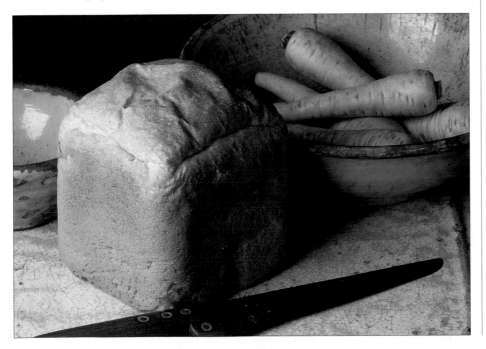

TROUBLESHOOTING

Bread machines are incredibly easy to use and, once you have become familiar with yours, you will wonder how you ever did without it. However, they are machines and they cannot think for themselves. Things can go wrong and you need to understand why. Here are a few handy troubleshooting tips.

BREAD RISES TOO MUCH

• Usually caused by too much yeast; reduce by 25 per cent.
• An excess of sugar will promote yeast action; try reducing the quantity of sugar.
• Did you leave out the salt or use less than was recommended? If so, the yeast would have been uncontrolled and a tall loaf would have been the likely result.
• Too much liquid can sometimes cause a loaf to over-rise. Try reducing by 15–30ml/ 1–2 tbsp next time.
• Other possibilities are too much dough or too hot a day.

BREAD DOES NOT RISE ENOUGH

• Insufficient yeast or yeast that is past its expiry date.
• A rapid cycle was chosen, giving the bread less time to rise.

• The yeast and salt came into contact with each other before mixing. Make sure they are placed in separate areas when added to the bread pan.
• Too much salt inhibits the action of the yeast. You may have added salt twice, or added other salty ingredients, such as ready-salted nuts or feta cheese.
• Wholegrain and wholemeal breads tend not to rise as high as white flour breads. These flours contain bran and wheat germ, which makes the flour heavier.
• You may have used a plain white flour instead of a strong bread flour, which has a higher gluten content.
• The ingredients were not at the correct temperature. If they were too hot, they may have killed the yeast; if they were too cold, they may have retarded the action of the yeast.
• Insufficient liquid. In order for dough to rise adequately, it needs to be soft and pliable. If the dough was dry and stiff, add more liquid next time.
• The lid was open during the rising stage for long enough to let warm air escape.
• No sugar was added. Yeast works better where there is at least 5ml/1 tsp sugar to feed it. Note, however, that high sugar levels may retard yeast action.

BREAD DOES NOT RISE AT ALL

• No yeast was added or it was past its expiry date.
• The yeast was not handled correctly and was probably killed by adding ingredients that were too hot.

THE DOUGH IS CRUMBLY AND DOESN'T FORM A BALL

• The dough is too dry. Add extra liquid a small amount at a time until the ingredients combine to form a pliable dough.

THE DOUGH IS VERY STICKY AND DOESN'T FORM A BALL

• The dough is too wet. Try adding a little extra flour, a spoonful at a time, waiting for it to be absorbed before adding more. You must do this while the machine is still mixing and kneading the dough.

BREAD MIXED BUT NOT BAKED

• A dough cycle was selected. Remove the dough, shape it and bake it in a conventional oven or bake it in the machine on the "bake only" cycle.

BREAD COLLAPSED AFTER RISING OR DURING BAKING

• Too much liquid was added. Reduce the amount by 15–30ml/1–2 tbsp next time, or add a little extra flour.
• The bread rose too much. Reduce the amount of yeast slightly in the future, or use a quicker cycle.
• Insufficient salt. Salt helps to prevent the dough from over-proving.
• The machine may have been placed in a draught or may have been knocked or jolted during rising.
• High humidity and warm weather may have caused the dough to rise too fast.
• Too much yeast may have been added.
• The dough may have contained a high proportion of cheese.

THERE ARE DEPOSITS OF FLOUR ON THE SIDES OF THE LOAF

• The dry ingredients, especially the flour, stuck to the sides of the pan during kneading, and then adhered to the rising dough. Next time, use a flexible rubber spatula to scrape down the sides of the pan after 5–10 minutes of the initial mixing cycle, if necessary, but take care to avoid the kneading blade.

CRUST IS SHRIVELLED OR WRINKLED

• Moisture condensed on top of the loaf while it was cooling. Remove from the bread machine as soon as it is cooled.

CRUMBLY, COARSE TEXTURE

• The bread rose too much; try reducing the quantity of yeast slightly next time.
• The dough didn't have enough liquid.
• Too many whole grains were added. These soaked up the liquid. Next time, either soak the whole grains in water first or increase the general liquid content.

BURNT CRUST

• There was too much sugar in the dough. Use less or try a light crust setting for sweet breads.
• Choose the sweet bread setting if the machine has this option.

PALE LOAF

• Add milk, either dried or fresh, to the dough. This encourages browning.
• Set the crust colour to dark.
• Increase the sugar slightly.

CRUST TOO CHEWY AND TOUGH

• Increase the butter or oil and milk.

BREAD NOT BAKED IN THE CENTRE OR ON TOP

• Too much liquid was added; next time, reduce the liquid by 15ml/1 tbsp or add a little extra flour.
• The quantities were too large and your machine could not cope with the dough.
• The dough was too rich; it contained too much fat, sugar, eggs, nuts or grains.
• The bread machine lid was not closed properly, or the machine was used in too cold a location.
• The flour may have been too heavy. This can occur when you use rye, bran and whole-meal (whole-wheat) flours. Replace some of it with white bread flour next time.

CRUST TOO SOFT OR CRISP

• For a softer crust, increase the fat and use milk instead of water. For a crisper crust, do the opposite.
• Use the French bread setting for a crisper crust.
• Keep a crisper crust by lifting the bread out of the pan and turn it out on to a wire rack as soon as the baking cycle finishes.

AIR BUBBLE UNDER THE CRUST

• The dough was not mixed well or didn't deflate properly during the knock-down cycle between risings. This is likely to be a one-off problem, but if it persists, try adding an extra spoonful of water.

ADDED INGREDIENTS WERE CHOPPED UP INSTEAD OF REMAINING WHOLE

• They were added too soon and were chopped by the kneading blade. Add on the machine's audible signal, or 5 minutes before the end of the kneading cycle.
• Leave chopped nuts and dried fruits in larger pieces.

ADDED INGREDIENTS NOT MIXED IN

• They were probably added too late in the kneading cycle. Next time, add them a couple of minutes sooner.

THE BREAD IS DRY

• The bread was left uncovered to cool too long and dried out.
• Breads low in fat dry out rapidly. Increase the fat or oil in the recipe.
• The bread was stored in the refrigerator. Next time place in a plastic bag when cool and store in a bread bin.

BREAD HAS A HOLEY TEXTURE

• The dough was too wet; use less liquid.
• Salt was omitted.
• Warm weather and/or high humidity caused the dough to rise too quickly.

A STICKY LAYERED UNRISEN MESS

• You forgot to put the kneading blade in the pan before adding the ingredients.
• The kneading blade was not correctly inserted on the shaft.
• The bread pan was incorrectly fitted.

SMOKE EMITTED FROM THE MACHINE

• Ingredients were spilt on the heating element. Remove the bread pan before adding ingredients, and add any extra ingredients carefully.

OTHER FACTORS

Creating the ideal conditions for your bread machine is largely a matter of trial and error. Take into account the time of year, the humidity and your altitude. Bread machines vary between models and manufacturers, and flour and yeast may produce slightly different results from brand to brand or country to country. Breads made in Australia, for example, often need slightly more water than those made in Britain.

You will soon get to know your machine. Watch the dough as it is mixing and check again before it begins to bake. Make a note of any tendencies (do you generally need to add more flour? does the bread often over-rise?) and adapt recipes accordingly.

BASIC BREADS

These recipes are the everyday breads that you will want to make time and again. They are some of the easiest breads to make in your machine; perfect for serving toasted with lashings of butter or for use in sandwiches. They include breads made from a wide range of flours, including bulgur wheat, buckwheat and spelt, as well as breads enriched with potato or egg. If you haven't made bread in your machine before, this is the place to start.

FARMHOUSE LOAF

The flour-dusted split top gives a charmingly rustic look to this tasty wholemeal-enriched white loaf.

SMALL

210ml/7½fl oz/scant 1 cup water
350g/12oz/3 cups unbleached white bread flour, plus extra for dusting
25g/1oz/¼ cup wholemeal (whole-wheat) bread flour
15ml/1 tbsp skimmed milk powder (non fat dry milk)
7.5ml/1½ tsp salt
7.5ml/1½ tsp granulated sugar
15g/½oz/1 tbsp butter
4ml/¾ tsp easy bake (rapid-rise) dried yeast
water, for glazing

MEDIUM

320ml/11¼fl oz/generous 1⅓ cups water
425g/15oz/3¾ cups unbleached white bread flour, plus extra for dusting
75g/3oz/¾ cup wholemeal bread flour
22ml/1½ tbsp skimmed milk powder
7.5ml/1½ tsp salt
7.5ml/1½ tsp granulated sugar
25g/1oz/2 tbsp butter
5ml/1 tsp easy bake dried yeast
water, for glazing

LARGE

375ml/13½fl oz/1½ cups + 1 tbsp water
525g/1lb 3oz/4¾ cups unbleached white bread flour, plus extra for dusting
75g/3oz/⅔ cup wholemeal bread flour
30ml/2 tbsp skimmed milk powder
10ml/2 tsp salt
10ml/2 tsp granulated sugar
25g/1oz/2 tbsp butter
7.5ml/1½ tsp easy bake dried yeast
water, for glazing

MAKES 1 LOAF

1 Pour the water into the bread pan. If the instructions for your machine specify that the yeast is to be placed in the pan first, reverse the order in which you add the liquid and dry ingredients. Sprinkle over both the flours, covering the water completely. Add the milk powder. Add the salt, sugar and butter in separate corners. Make a small indent in the centre of the flour (but not down as far as the liquid) and add the yeast.

2 Set the bread machine to the white/basic setting, medium crust. Size: 500g for small, large/750g for medium or 1kg/2lb for large. Press Start.

4 Remove the bread at the end of the baking cycle and turn out on to a wire rack to cool.

3 Ten minutes before the baking time commences, brush the top of the loaf with water and dust with white bread flour. Slash the top with a sharp knife.

COOK'S TIP
Try this rustic bread using Granary or Malthouse flour instead of wholemeal bread flour for added texture.

Per loaf Energy 1457kcal/6180kJ; Protein 39.5g; Carbohydrate 300.8g, of which sugars 18.6g; Fat 19.1g, of which saturates 9.9g; Cholesterol 40mg; Calcium 626mg; Fibre 13.1g; Sodium 3127mg.

EGG-ENRICHED WHITE LOAF

Adding egg to a basic white loaf gives a richer flavour and creamier crumb, as well as a wonderfully golden finish to the crust.

1 Put the egg(s) in a measuring jug (cup) and add sufficient water to give 240ml/ 8½fl oz/generous 1 cup, 300ml/10½fl oz/ 1⅓ cups or 385ml/13¼fl oz/1⅚ cups, according to the size of loaf selected.

2 Mix lightly and pour into the bread machine pan. If your instructions specify that the yeast is to be placed in the pan first, reverse the order in which you add the liquid and the dry ingredients.

SMALL
1 egg
water, see method
375g/13oz/3¼ cups unbleached white
bread flour
7.5ml/1½ tsp granulated sugar
7.5ml/1½ tsp salt
20g/¾oz/1½ tbsp butter
4ml/¾ tsp easy bake (rapid-rise)
dried yeast

MEDIUM
1 egg plus 1 egg yolk
water, see method
500g/1lb 2oz/4½ cups unbleached
white bread flour
10ml/2 tsp granulated sugar
7.5ml/1½ tsp salt
25g/1oz/2 tbsp butter
5ml/1 tsp easy bake dried yeast

LARGE
2 eggs
water, see method
600g/1lb 5oz/5¼ cups unbleached
white bread flour
10ml/2 tsp granulated sugar
7.5ml/1½ tsp salt
25g/1oz/2 tbsp butter
7.5ml/1½ tsp easy bake dried yeast

MAKES 1 LOAF

3 Sprinkle over the flour, covering the water. In separate corners of the pan, add the sugar, salt and butter. Make an indent in the centre of the flour. Add the yeast.

4 Set the bread machine to the white/ basic setting, medium crust. Size: 500g for small, large/750g for medium or 1kg/2lb for large. Press Start. At the end of the cycle, turn out on to a wire rack.

Per loaf Energy 1529kcal/6476kJ; Protein 41.6g; Carbohydrate 299.2g, of which sugars 13.5g; Fat 26.8g, of which saturates 13.1g; Cholesterol 236mg; Calcium 561mg; Fibre 11.6g; Sodium 3179mg.

MALTED LOAF

A malt and sultana loaf makes the perfect breakfast or tea-time treat.
Serve it sliced and generously spread with butter.

SMALL
210ml/7½fl oz/scant 1 cup water
15ml/1 tbsp golden (light corn) syrup
22ml/1½ tbsp malt extract
375g/13oz/3¼ cups unbleached white bread flour
22ml/1½ tbsp skimmed milk powder (non fat dry milk)
2.5ml/½ tsp salt
40g/1½oz/3 tbsp butter
2.5ml/½ tsp easy bake (rapid-rise) dried yeast
75g/3oz/½ cup sultanas (golden raisins)

MEDIUM
280ml/10fl oz/1¼ cups water
22ml/1½ tbsp golden syrup
30ml/2 tbsp malt extract
500g/1lb 2oz/4½ cups unbleached white bread flour
30ml/2 tbsp skimmed milk powder
5ml/1 tsp salt
50g/2oz/¼ cup butter
5ml/1 tsp easy bake dried yeast
100g/3½oz/generous ½ cup sultanas

LARGE
320ml/11fl oz/generous 1⅓ cups water
30ml/2 tbsp golden syrup
45ml/3 tbsp malt extract
600g/1lb 5oz/5¼ cups unbleached white bread flour
30ml/2 tbsp skimmed milk powder
5ml/1 tsp salt
50g/2oz/¼ cup butter
7.5ml/1½ tsp easy bake dried yeast
125g/4½oz/generous ⅔ cup sultanas

MAKES 1 LOAF

1 Pour the water, golden syrup and malt extract into the bread machine pan. If the instructions for your machine specify that the yeast is to be placed in the pan first, reverse the order in which you add the liquid and dry ingredients.

2 Sprinkle over the flour so that it covers the liquid. Add the milk powder. Add the salt and butter in separate corners. Make a shallow indent in the centre of the flour and add the yeast.

3 Set the machine to the white/basic setting, raisin setting if available. Select light crust, 500g for small; medium crust, large/750g for medium; or medium crust 1kg/2lb for large. Add the sultanas to the automatic dispenser, if available, or when the machine beeps during the kneading cycle. Press Start.

4 Remove the loaf at the end of the baking cycle and turn out on to a wire rack.

5 Glaze the bread immediately, if you like, by dissolving 15ml/1 tbsp caster (superfine) sugar in 15ml/1 tbsp milk and brushing over the top crust. Allow to cool.

Per loaf Energy 1876kcal/7938kJ; Protein 37.5g; Carbohydrate 368.9g, of which sugars 83.1g; Fat 37.9g, of which saturates 22.4g; Cholesterol 92mg; Calcium 676mg; Fibre 13.1g; Sodium 1401mg.

LIGHT WHOLEMEAL BREAD

—

*A tasty, light wholemeal loaf, which can be cooked on the quicker basic
or normal setting of your bread machine.*

SMALL
*280ml/10fl oz/1¼ cups water
250g/9oz/2¼ cups wholemeal
(whole-wheat) bread flour
125g/4½oz/generous 1 cup white
bread flour
15ml/1 tbsp skimmed milk powder
7.5ml/1½ tsp salt
7.5ml/1½ tsp granulated sugar
20g/¾oz/1½ tbsp butter
5ml/1 tsp easy bake (rapid-rise)
dried yeast*

MEDIUM
*350ml/12fl oz/1½ cups water
350g/12oz/3 cups wholemeal bread flour
150g/5½oz/1⅓ cups white bread flour
30ml/2 tbsp skimmed milk powder
7.5ml/1½ tsp salt
10ml/2 tsp granulated sugar
25g/1oz/2 tbsp butter
7.5ml/1½ tsp easy bake dried yeast*

LARGE
*400ml/14fl oz/scant 1¾ cups water
425g/15oz/3¾ cups wholemeal
bread flour
175g/6oz/generous 1½ cups white
bread flour
30ml/2 tbsp skimmed milk powder
10ml/2 tsp salt
15ml/1 tbsp granulated sugar
25g/1oz/2 tbsp butter
7.5ml/1½ tsp easy bake dried yeast*

MAKES 1 LOAF

VARIATION
Another option for a lighter brown
bread is to replace the wholemeal
bread flour with brown bread flour.
This contains less bran and wheatgerm
than wholemeal flour, making it lighter.

1 Pour the water into the bread machine pan. If the instructions for your bread machine specify that the yeast is to be placed in the pan first, reverse the order in which you add the liquid and dry ingredients to the pan.

2 Sprinkle over both flours ensuring that the water is completely covered. Add the skimmed milk powder. Add the salt, sugar and butter in separate corners of the bread pan. Make a small indent in the centre of the flour and add the yeast.

3 Set the bread machine to the white/basic setting, medium or light crust. Size: 500g for small, large/750g for medium or 1kg/2lb for large. Press Start.

4 Remove the bread at the end of the baking cycle. Turn out on to a wire rack.

Per loaf Energy 1277kcal/5429kJ; Protein 46.8g; Carbohydrate 269.7g, of which sugars 20g; Fat 8.8g, of which saturates 2g; Cholesterol 6mg; Calcium 395mg; Fibre 26.4g; Sodium 3014mg.

FRENCH BREAD

French bread traditionally has a crisp crust and light, chewy crumb. Use the special French bread setting on your bread machine to help to achieve this unique texture.

SMALL
MAKES 1 LOAF
150ml/5fl oz/⅔ cup water
225g/8oz/2 cups unbleached white bread flour
5ml/1 tsp salt
7.5ml/1½ tsp easy bake (rapid-rise) dried yeast

MEDIUM
MAKES 2–3 LOAVES
315ml/11fl oz/1⅓ cups water
450g/1lb/4 cups unbleached white bread flour
7.5ml/1½ tsp salt
7.5ml/1½ tsp easy bake dried yeast

LARGE
MAKES 3–4 LOAVES
500ml/17½fl oz/2⅛ cups water
675g/1½lb/6 cups unbleached white bread flour
10ml/2 tsp salt
10ml/2 tsp easy bake dried yeast

1 Add the water to the bread machine pan. If the instructions for your machine specify that the yeast is to be placed in the pan first, reverse the order in which you add the liquid and dry ingredients.

2 Sprinkle the flour over the water. Add the salt in a corner. Make an indent in the centre of the flour and add the yeast. Use the French dough/Artisan dough setting (see Cook's Tip). Press Start.

3 When the dough cycle has finished, remove the dough from the machine, place it on a lightly floured surface and knock it back (punch it down). Divide it into two or three equal portions if using the medium quantities or three or four portions if using the large quantities.

4 On a floured surface shape each piece of dough into a ball, then roll out to a rectangle measuring 18–20 × 7.5cm/ 7–8 × 3in. Fold one-third up lengthways and one-third down, then press. Repeat twice more, leaving the dough to rest between foldings to avoid tearing.

5 Gently roll and stretch each piece to a 28–33cm/11–13in loaf, depending on whether you aim to make smaller or larger loaves. Place each loaf in a floured banneton or between the folds of a floured and pleated dishtowel, so that the French bread shape is maintained during rising.

6 Cover with lighly oiled clear film (plastic wrap) and leave in a warm place for 30–45 minutes. Preheat the oven to 230°C/450°F/Gas 8.

7 Roll the loaf or loaves on to a baking sheet, spaced well part. Slash the tops with a knife. Place at the top of the oven, spray the inside of the oven with water and bake for 15–20 minutes, or until golden. Transfer to a wire rack.

COOK'S TIP
Use the French bread baking setting if you do not have a French bread dough setting. Remove the dough before the final rising stage and shape as directed.

Per loaf Energy 767kcal/3263kJ; Protein 21.1g; Carbohydrate 174.8g, of which sugars 3.4g; Fat 2.9g, of which saturates 0.5g; Cholesterol 0mg; Calcium 316mg; Fibre 7g; Sodium 1972mg.

POTATO BREAD

This golden crusty loaf has a moist soft centre and is perfect for sandwiches.
Use the water in which the potatoes have been cooked to make this bread.
If you haven't got enough, make up the remainder with tap water.

1 Pour the water and sunflower oil into the bread machine pan. However, if the instructions for your machine specify that the yeast is to be placed in the pan first, reverse the order in which you add the liquid and dry ingredients.

2 Sprinkle over the flour, ensuring that it covers the water. Add the mashed potato and milk powder. Add the salt and sugar in separate corners of the bread pan. Make a small indent in the centre of the flour (but not down as far as the liquid) and add the yeast.

3 Set the bread machine to the white/basic setting, medium or light crust. Size: 500g for small, large/750g for medium or 1kg/2lb for large. Press Start. To glaze the loaf, brush with the top of the milk halfway through the cooking time.

4 Remove the bread at the end of the baking cycle. Turn out on to a wire rack.

SMALL
200ml/7fl oz/⅞ cup potato cooking water, at room temperature
30ml/2 tbsp sunflower oil
375g/13oz/3¼ cups unbleached white bread flour
125g/4½oz/1½ cups cold mashed potato
15ml/1 tbsp skimmed milk powder (non fat dry milk)
5ml/1 tsp salt
7.5ml/1½ tsp granulated sugar
5ml/1 tsp easy bake (rapid-rise) dried yeast
milk, for glazing

MEDIUM
240ml/8½fl oz/generous 1 cup potato cooking water, at room temperature
30ml/2 tbsp sunflower oil
500g/1lb 2oz/4½ cups unbleached white bread flour
175g/6oz/2 cups cold mashed potato
22ml/1½ tbsp skimmed milk powder
7.5ml/1½ tsp salt
10ml/2 tsp granulated sugar
7.5ml/1½ tsp easy bake dried yeast
milk, for glazing

LARGE
290ml/generous ½ pint/scant 1¼ cups potato cooking water, at room temperature
45ml/3 tbsp sunflower oil
600g/1lb/5¼ cups unbleached white bread flour
200g/7oz/scant 2½ cups cold cooked mashed potato
30ml/2 tbsp skimmed milk powder
7.5ml/1½ tsp salt
15ml/1 tbsp granulated sugar
7.5ml/1½ tsp easy bake dried yeast
milk, for glazing

MAKES 1 LOAF

COOK'S TIP
If using leftover potatoes mashed with milk and butter you may need to reduce the liquid. If making the mashed potato, use 175g/6oz, 200g/7oz or 250g/9oz raw potatoes, depending on machine size.

Per loaf Energy 1643kcal/6953kJ; Protein 38g; Carbohydrate 319.3g, of which sugars 15.5g; Fat 32.5g, of which saturates 7g; Cholesterol 16mg; Calcium 564mg; Fibre 13g; Sodium 2039mg.

CORN MEAL BREAD

This scrumptious bread has a sweet flavour and crumbly texture. Use a finely ground corn meal (also known as maize meal) from the health-food store. The coarsely ground meal used for polenta makes a good topping.

SMALL

150ml/5fl oz/⅔ cup warm water
85ml/3fl oz/5 tbsp lukewarm milk
15ml/1 tbsp corn oil
275g/10oz/2½ cups unbleached white bread flour
100g/3½oz/scant 1 cup corn meal
5ml/1 tsp salt
7.5ml/1½ tsp light muscovado (brown) sugar
5ml/1 tsp easy bake (rapid-rise) dried yeast
water, for glazing
polenta, for sprinkling

MEDIUM

210ml/7½fl oz/scant 1 cup warm water
90ml/3fl oz/6 tbsp lukewarm milk
22ml/1½ tbsp corn oil
350g/12½oz/3 cups unbleached white bread flour
150g/5oz/1¼ cups corn meal
5ml/1 tsp salt
10ml/2 tsp light muscovado sugar
5ml/1 tsp easy bake dried yeast
water, for glazing
polenta, for sprinkling

LARGE

225ml/8fl oz/scant 1 cup warm water
140ml/5fl oz/⅝ cup lukewarm milk
30ml/2 tbsp corn oil
400g/14oz/3½ cups unbleached white bread flour
200g/7oz/1¾ cups corn meal
7.5ml/1½ tsp salt
10ml/2 tsp light muscovado sugar
7.5ml/1½ tsp easy bake dried yeast
water, for glazing
polenta, for sprinkling

MAKES 1 LOAF

COOK'S TIP

This bread is best cooked on a rapid setting, even though corn meal gives a slightly shallow loaf. If the rapid programme is less than 1 hour 50 minutes use warm milk and water to help the performance of the yeast.

1 Pour the water, milk and corn oil into the pan. Reverse the order in which you add the wet and dry ingredients if the instructions to your machine specify this.

2 Add the flour and the corn meal, covering the water. Place the salt and sugar in separate corners. Make a shallow indent in the flour; add the yeast.

3 Set the bread machine to the white rapid/basic rapid/fastbake setting, medium crust. Size: 500g for small, large/750g for medium or 1kg/2lb for large. Press Start. Just before the baking cycle starts, brush loaf with water and sprinkle with polenta.

4 Remove the bread at the end of the baking cycle. Turn out on to a wire rack.

Per loaf Energy 1473kcal/6226kJ; Protein 38.1g; Carbohydrate 298.9g, of which sugars 16.2g; Fat 19.3g, of which saturates 2.5g; Cholesterol 5mg; Calcium 494mg; Fibre 10.7g; Sodium 2020mg.

WHOLEMEAL BREAD

This is a hearty bread with a full nutty flavour and coarse texture from the wheatgerm and bran found in the wholemeal flour.

SMALL

280ml/10fl oz/1 cup + 3 tbsp water
10ml/2 tsp lemon juice
385g/13½ oz/3⅜ cups wholemeal
(whole-wheat) bread flour
20g/¾ oz/1½ tbsp butter
7.5ml/1½ tsp salt
7.5ml/1½ tsp sugar
5ml/1 tsp easy bake (rapid-rise)
dried yeast

MEDIUM

350ml/12fl oz/1½ cups water
10ml/2 tsp lemon juice
500g/1lb 2oz/ 4½ cups wholemeal
bread flour
25g/1oz/2 tbsp butter
10ml/2 tsp salt
10ml/2 tsp sugar
5ml/1 tsp easy bake dried yeast

LARGE

380ml/13½fl oz/1⅝ cups water
15ml/1 tbsp lemon juice
600g/1lb 5oz/5¼ cups wholemeal
bread flour
25g/1oz/2 tbsp butter
10ml/2 tsp salt
15ml/1 tbsp sugar
6.5ml/1⅓ tsp easy bake dried yeast

MAKES 1 LOAF

3 Set the bread machine to the whole wheat setting, medium crust, if available. Size: 500g for small, large/750g for medium or 1kg/2lb for large. Press Start.

4 Remove the bread from the bread pan at the end of the baking cycle, then turn it out on to a wire rack to cool.

COOK'S TIP
Depending on the gluten strength of the flour, some bread machines work better if vitamin C is added to the dough. If your loaf over-rises and collapses slightly, try adding 1 x 100mg vitamin C tablet, crushed, to the flour in step 2.

1 Pour the water into the bread machine pan. Add the lemon juice. If the instructions for your machine specify that the yeast is to be placed in the pan first, reverse the order in which you add the liquid and the dry ingredients.

2 Sprinkle over the flour, ensuring that it covers the water. Add the butter, salt and sugar in separate corners of the bread pan. Make a small indent in the centre of the flour (but not down as far as the liquid) and add the yeast.

Per loaf Energy 1370kcal/5807kJ; Protein 49g; Carbohydrate 253.9g, of which sugars 15.9g; Fat 24.8g, of which saturates 12g; Cholesterol 46mg; Calcium 154mg; Fibre 34.6g; Sodium 3110mg.

SPELT AND BULGUR WHEAT BREAD

Two unusual grains are used here. The bulgur wheat contributes crunch while the spelt flour adds a nutty flavour.

SMALL
110ml/scant 4fl oz/scant ½ cup water
100ml/3½fl oz/7 tbsp buttermilk
5ml/1 tsp lemon juice
250g/9oz/2¼ cups unbleached white
bread flour
100g/3½oz/scant 1 cup spelt flour
30ml/2 tbsp bulgur wheat
5ml/1 tsp salt
10ml/2 tsp granulated sugar
5ml/1 tsp easy bake (rapid-rise) dried
yeast

MEDIUM
220ml/scant 8fl oz/scant 1 cup water
125ml/4½fl oz/generous ½ cup
buttermilk
7.5ml/1½ tsp lemon juice
350g/12oz/3 cups unbleached white
bread flour
150g/5½oz/1⅓ cups spelt flour
45ml/3 tbsp bulgur wheat
7.5ml/1½ tsp salt
15ml/1 tbsp granulated sugar
7.5ml/1½ tsp easy bake dried yeast

LARGE
250ml/9fl oz/generous 1 cup water
125ml/4⅓fl oz/generous ½ cup
buttermilk
10ml/2 tsp lemon juice
375g/13oz/3¼ cups unbleached white
bread flour
175g/6oz/generous 1½ cups spelt flour
60ml/4 tbsp bulgur wheat
10ml/2 tsp salt
15ml/1 tbsp granulated sugar
7.5ml/1½ tsp easy bake dried yeast

MAKES 1 LOAF

VARIATION
The buttermilk adds a characteristic slightly sour note to this bread. You can replace it with low-fat natural (plain) yogurt or semi-skimmed (low-fat) milk for a less tangy flavour.

2 Sprinkle over both types of flour, then the bulgur wheat, ensuring that the liquid is completely covered. Add the salt and sugar, placing them in separate corners of the bread pan.

3 Make a small indent in the centre of the flour (but not down as far as the liquid) and add the yeast.

4 Set the machine to the white/basic setting, medium crust. Size: 500g for small, large/750g for medium or 1kg/2lb for large. Press Start.

5 Remove the bread at the end of the cycle and turn out on to a wire rack.

1 Pour the water, buttermilk and lemon juice into the bread machine pan. If the instructions for your machine specify that the yeast is to be placed in the pan first, reverse the order in which you add the liquid and dry ingredients.

Per loaf Energy 1341kcal/5695kJ; Protein 42.5g; Carbohydrate 296.5g, of which sugars 21.3g; Fat 6.3g, of which saturates 0.9g; Cholesterol 4mg; Calcium 527mg; Fibre 16.8g; Sodium 2032mg.

BUCKWHEAT AND WALNUT BREAD

Buckwheat flour has a distinctive earthy taste, perfectly mellowed when blended with white flour and walnuts in this compact bread, flavoured with molasses.

SMALL
210ml/7½fl oz/scant 1 cup water
10ml/2 tsp molasses
30ml/2 tbsp walnut or olive oil
325g/11½oz/scant 3 cups unbleached white bread flour
50g/2oz/½ cup buckwheat flour
15ml/1 tbsp skimmed milk powder (non fat dry milk)
5ml/1 tsp salt
2.5ml/½ tsp granulated sugar
5ml/1 tsp easy bake (rapid-rise) dried yeast
40g/1½oz/⅓ cup walnut pieces

MEDIUM
315ml/11fl oz/1⅜ cups water
15ml/3 tsp molasses
30ml/2 tbsp walnut or olive oil
425g/15oz/3¾ cups unbleached white bread flour
75g/3oz/¾ cup buckwheat flour
22ml/1½ tbsp skimmed milk powder
7.5ml/1½ tsp salt
4ml/¾ tsp granulated sugar
5ml/1 tsp easy bake dried yeast
50g/2oz/½ cup walnut pieces

LARGE
360ml/12¾fl oz/generous 1½ cups water
20ml/4 tsp molasses
45ml/3 tbsp walnut or olive oil
500g/1lb 2oz/4½ cups unbleached white bread flour
100g/3½oz/scant 1 cup buckwheat flour
30ml/2 tbsp skimmed milk powder
10ml/2 tsp salt
5ml/1 tsp granulated sugar
7.5ml/1½ tsp easy bake dried yeast
65g/2½oz/⅝ cup walnut pieces

MAKES 1 LOAF

1 Pour the water, molasses and walnut or olive oil into the bread pan. If the instructions for your machine specify that the yeast is to be placed in the pan first, reverse the order in which you add the liquid and dry ingredients.

2 Sprinkle over the flours, covering the liquid. Add the milk powder. Place the salt and sugar in separate corners. Make a small indent in the centre of the flour (but not down as far as the liquid) and add the easy bake dried yeast.

3 Set the machine to white/basic, raisin setting (if available), medium crust. Size: 500g for small, large/750g for medium or 1kg/2lb for large. Add the walnuts to the automatic dispenser, if available. Press Start. If adding manually, do so when the machine beeps during the kneading cycle, or after the first kneading. Remove the bread at the end of the baking cycle and turn on to a wire rack to cool.

Per loaf Energy 1825kcal/7690kJ; Protein 45.2g; Carbohydrate 310.3g, of which sugars 22.4g; Fat 53.5g, of which saturates 6.6g; Cholesterol 6mg; Calcium 488mg; Fibre 2.5g; Sodium 2082mg.

260ml/9fl oz/scant 1⅛ cups water
30ml/2 tbsp sunflower oil
15ml/1 tbsp clear honey
300g/10½oz/2⅔ cups unbleached
white bread flour
75g/3oz/¾ cup wholemeal
(whole-wheat) bread flour
150g/5½oz/1½ cups unsweetened fruit
and nut muesli (granola)
45ml/3 tbsp skimmed milk powder
(non fat dry milk)
7.5ml/1½ tsp salt
7.5ml/1½ tsp easy bake (rapid-rise)
dried yeast
65g/2½oz/scant ½ cup stoned (pitted)
dates, chopped

MAKES 1 LOAF

1 Pour the water, oil and honey into the bread pan. Reverse the order in which you add the wet and dry ingredients if necessary. Sprinkle over the flours, covering the water. Add the muesli and milk powder, then the salt, in a corner.

MUESLI AND DATE BREAD

This makes the perfect breakfast or brunch bread. Use your own favourite unsweetened muesli to ring the changes.

2 Make a small indent in the flour; add the yeast. Set to the dough setting; use basic raisin dough setting (if available). Press Start. Add the dates at the beep or during the last 5 minutes of kneading. Lightly oil a baking sheet.

3 When the dough cycle has finished, remove from the machine and place it on a surface dusted with wholemeal flour. Knock back (punch down) gently.

4 Shape the dough into a plump round and place it on the prepared baking sheet. Using a sharp knife make three cuts on the top about 1cm/½in deep, to divide the bread into six sections.

5 Cover the loaf with lightly oiled clear film (plastic wrap) and leave for 30–45 minutes, or until almost doubled in size.

6 Preheat the oven to 200°C/400°F/ Gas 6. Bake the loaf for 30–35 minutes until it is golden and hollow sounding. Transfer it to a wire rack to cool.

> **COOK'S TIP**
> The amount of water required may vary with the type of muesli used. Add another 15ml/1 tbsp water if the dough is too firm.

BARLEY-ENRICHED FARMHOUSE LOAF

Barley adds a very distinctive, earthy, slightly nutty flavour to this crusty white loaf.

260ml/9fl oz/1⅛ cups water
45ml/3 tbsp double (heavy) cream
400g/14oz/3½ cups unbleached white
bread flour
115g/4oz/1 cup barley flour
10ml/2 tsp granulated sugar
10ml/2 tsp salt
7.5ml/1½ tsp easy bake (rapid-rise)
dried yeast
25g/1oz/2 tbsp pumpkin seeds
flour, for dusting

MAKES 1 LOAF

1 Pour the water and cream into the pan. Reverse the order in which you add the liquid and dry ingredients if necessary. Sprinkle over both types of flour, covering the water completely. Add the sugar and salt, placing them in separate corners of the pan. Make a shallow indent in the centre of the flour and add the yeast.

2 Set the bread machine to the dough setting; use basic raisin dough setting (if available). Press Start. Add the pumpkin seeds when the machine beeps or during the last 5 minutes of kneading. Lightly oil a 900g/2lb loaf tin (pan) measuring 18.5 × 12cm/7¼ × 4½in.

3 When the dough cycle has finished, remove the dough from the machine and place on a lightly floured surface. Knock back (punch down) gently. Shape the dough into a rectangle, making the longer side the same length as the tin.

4 Roll the dough up lengthways, and tuck the ends under. Place it in the prepared tin, with the seam underneath. Cover with oiled clear film (plastic wrap) and leave for 30–45 minutes, or until the dough reaches the top of the tin.

5 Dust the loaf with flour then make a deep lengthways cut along the top. Leave to rest for 10 minutes. Preheat the oven to 220°C/425°F/Gas 7.

6 Bake the loaf for 15 minutes, then reduce the oven temperature to 200°C/ 400°F/Gas 6 and bake for 20–25 minutes more, or until the bread is golden and sounds hollow when tapped on the base. Transfer it to a wire rack to cool.

Per loaf Energy 2852kcal/12101kJ; Protein 65.9g; Carbohydrate 587.6g, of which sugars 197.4g; Fat 42.6g, of which saturates 7.4g; Cholesterol 9mg; Calcium 807mg; Fibre 31.6g; Sodium 3136mg.
Per loaf Energy 2143kcal/9070kJ; Protein 54.2g; Carbohydrate 416.5g, of which sugars 19.8g; Fat 42.7g, of which saturates 15.7g; Cholesterol 59mg; Calcium 777mg; Fibre 17.5g; Sodium 3963mg.

BRAN AND YOGURT BREAD

This soft-textured yogurt bread is enriched with bran. It is high in fibre and makes wonderful toast.

SMALL

150ml/5fl oz/⅔ cup water

125ml/4½fl oz/generous ½ cup natural (plain) yogurt

15ml/1 tbsp sunflower oil

15ml/1 tbsp molasses

200g/7oz/1¾ cups unbleached white bread flour

150g/5½oz/1⅓ cups wholemeal (whole-wheat) bread flour

25g/1oz/⅓ cup wheat bran

5ml/1 tsp salt

4ml/¾ tsp easy bake (rapid-rise) dried yeast

MEDIUM

185ml/6½fl oz/generous ¾ cup water

175ml/6fl oz/¾ cup natural yogurt

22ml/1½ tbsp sunflower oil

30ml/2 tbsp molasses

260g/generous 9oz/2⅓ cups unbleached white bread flour

200g/7oz/1¾ cups wholemeal bread flour

40g/1½oz/½ cup wheat bran

7.5ml/1½ tsp salt

5ml/1 tsp easy bake dried yeast

LARGE

200ml/7fl oz/⅞ cup water

190ml/6¾fl oz/scant ⅞ cup natural yogurt

30ml/2 tbsp sunflower oil

30ml/2 tbsp molasses

340g/12oz/3 cups unbleached white bread flour

225g/8oz/2 cups wholemeal bread flour

40g/½oz/⅔ cup wheat bran

10ml/2 tsp salt

7.5ml/1½ tsp easy bake dried yeast

MAKES 1 LOAF

1 Pour the water, yogurt, oil and molasses into the bread machine pan. If the instructions for your machine specify that the yeast is to be placed in the pan first, reverse the order in which you add the liquid and dry ingredients.

2 Sprinkle over both the white and the wholemeal flours, ensuring that the liquid mixture is completely covered. Add the wheat bran and salt, then make a small indent in the centre of the dry ingredients (but not down as far as the liquid) and add the easy bake dried yeast.

3 Set the bread machine to the white/basic setting, medium crust. Size: 500g for small, large/750g for medium or 1kg/2lb for large. Press Start.

4 Remove the bread from the pan at the end of the baking cycle and turn out on to a wire rack to cool. Serve when still just warm, if you like.

COOK'S TIP
Molasses is added to this bread to give added flavour and colour. You can use treacle or golden (light corn) syrup instead, to intensify or lessen the flavour respectively, if desired.

Per loaf Energy 1406kcal/5961kJ; Protein 47.9g; Carbohydrate 277.4g, of which sugars 26.6g; Fat 19.5g, of which saturates 3g; Cholesterol 2mg; Calcium 678mg; Fibre 28.8g; Sodium 2101mg.

APPLE AND CIDER SEEDED BREAD

This bread is perfect served with a selection of cold meats, paté or cheese for a delicious lunchtime spread.

SMALL
200ml/7fl oz/⅞ cup medium sweet cider, left to become flat
15ml/1 tbsp sunflower oil
115g/4oz/¾ cup finely chopped green eating apple
400g/14oz/3½ cups seeded white bread flour
15ml/1 tbsp skimmed milk powder (non fat dry milk)
5ml/1 tsp salt
7.5ml/1½ tsp sugar
5ml/1 tsp easy bake (rapid-rise) dried yeast

MEDIUM
260ml/9fl oz/1⅛ cups medium sweet cider, left to become flat
30ml/2 tbsp sunflower oil
125g/4½oz/1 cup finely chopped green eating apple
525g/1lb 3oz/4¾ cups seeded white bread flour
22ml/1½ tbsp skimmed milk powder
7.5ml/1½ tsp salt
7.5ml/1½ tsp sugar
5ml/1 tsp easy bake dried yeast

LARGE
320ml/11½fl oz/1⅓ cups medium sweet cider, left to become flat
30ml/2 tbsp sunflower oil
150g/5oz/generous 1 cup finely chopped green eating apple
625g/1lb 5oz/5½ cups seeded white bread flour
30ml/2 tbsp skimmed milk powder
7.5ml/1½ tsp salt
10ml/2 tsp sugar
7.5ml/1½ tsp easy bake dried yeast

MAKES 1 LOAF

1 Pour the cider into the bread machine pan. Add the sunflower oil and chopped apple. If the instructions for your machine specify that the yeast is to be placed in the pan first, reverse the order in which you add the liquid and the dry ingredients.

2 Sprinkle over the flour, ensuring that it covers the water. Add the skimmed milk powder, salt and sugar in separate corners of the bread pan. Make a small indent in the centre of the flour (but not down as far as the liquid) and add the yeast.

3 Set the bread machine to the white/basic setting, light crust. Size: 500g for small, large/750g for medium or 1kg/2lb for large. Press Start.

4 Remove the bread at the end of the baking cycle. Turn out on to a wire rack.

Per loaf Energy 1663kcal/7053kJ; Protein 41.3g; Carbohydrate 342.5g, of which sugars 37.7g; Fat 18g, of which saturates 3.1g; Cholesterol 6mg; Calcium 705mg; Fibre 14.2g; Sodium 2049mg.

SAVOURY BREADS

Adding flavourings to a basic dough provides many new ideas. Herbs, such as rosemary,

dill and sage, along with garlic and onion will fill the kitchen with delicious scents.

Cheeses such as mascarpone, Parmesan, Gorgonzola and mozzarella can be used to give

rich loaves with a wonderful aroma. You can also add meat or cooked vegetables to savoury

breads for a tasty flavour: try pumpkin, sweet potato or sun-dried tomatoes.

STROMBOLI

200ml/7fl oz/⅞ cup water
350g/12oz/3 cups unbleached white
bread flour
2.5ml/½ tsp granulated sugar
5ml/1 tsp salt
5ml/1 tsp easy bake (rapid-rise)
dried yeast

FOR THE FILLING
175g/6oz mozzarella cheese, grated or
finely chopped
75g/3oz/1 cup freshly grated
Parmesan cheese
15ml/1 tbsp chopped fresh parsley
30ml/2 tbsp fresh basil leaves
5ml/1 tsp freshly ground black pepper
1 garlic clove, finely chopped

FOR THE TOPPING
15ml/1 tbsp extra virgin olive oil
4–5 small fresh rosemary sprigs,
woody stems removed

MAKES 1 LOAF

This variation on Italian Focaccia takes its name from the volcanic island of Stromboli, near Sicily. The dough is pierced to allow the filling to "erupt" through the holes during baking. This bread can be served warm or cold.

1 Pour the water into the machine pan. Reverse the order in which you add the wet and dry ingredients if necessary. Sprinkle over the flour, ensuring that it covers the water. Add the sugar and salt in separate corners of the pan. Make a shallow indent in the centre of the flour and add the yeast.

2 Set the bread machine to the dough setting; use basic dough setting (if available). Press Start.

3 Lightly oil a baking sheet. When the dough cycle has ended, remove the dough and place on a lightly floured surface. Knock it back (punch it down) gently. Roll out into a rectangle 30 × 23cm/12 × 9in. Cover with oiled clear film (plastic wrap) and leave to rest for 5 minutes.

4 Sprinkle over the cheeses leaving a 1cm/½in clear border along each edge. Add the parsley, basil, pepper and garlic.

5 Starting from a shorter side, roll up the dough, Swiss roll fashion, tucking the side edges under to seal. Place the roll, seam down, on the baking sheet. Cover with lightly oiled clear film and leave in a warm place for 30 minutes, or until the dough roll has almost doubled in size.

6 Preheat the oven to 200°C/400°F/Gas 6. Brush the top of the bread with olive oil, then use a skewer to prick holes in the bread, from the top right through to the base. Sprinkle the rosemary over the bread. Bake for 30–35 minutes, or until the bread is golden. Transfer it to a wire rack.

THREE CHEESES BREAD

180ml/6½fl oz/generous ¾ cup water
1 egg
100g/3½oz/5 tbsp mascarpone cheese
400g/14oz/3½ cups unbleached white
bread flour
50g/2oz/½ cup Granary
(whole-wheat) flour
10ml/2 tsp granulated sugar
5ml/1 tsp salt
7.5ml/1½ tsp easy bake (rapid-rise)
dried yeast
75g/3oz Mountain Gorgonzola cheese,
cut into small dice
75g/3oz/1 cup freshly grated
Parmesan cheese
45ml/3 tbsp chopped fresh chives

FOR THE TOPPING
1 egg yolk
15ml/1 tbsp water
15ml/1 tbsp wheat flakes

MAKES 1 LOAF

A tempting trio of Italian cheeses – mascarpone, Gorgonzola and Parmesan – are responsible for the marvellous flavour of this round loaf.

1 Add the water, egg and mascarpone to the pan. Reverse the order in which you add the wet and dry ingredients if necessary. Sprinkle over both types of flour, covering the water completely. Add the sugar and salt in separate corners. Make a small indent in the flour; add the yeast. Set the machine to the dough setting; use basic raisin dough setting (if available). Press Start.

2 Add the Gorgonzola, Parmesan and chives as the machine beeps or during the last 5 minutes of kneading. Lightly oil a baking sheet.

3 When the dough cycle has finished, place the dough on a floured surface. Knock back (punch down) gently, then shape it into a round loaf, about 20cm/8in in diameter.

4 Cover with oiled clear film (plastic wrap); leave in a warm place for 30–45 minutes. Preheat the oven to 200°C/400°F/Gas 6.

5 Mix the egg yolk and water together and brush this glaze over the top of the bread. Sprinkle with wheat flakes. Score the top of the bread into eight equal segments. Bake for 30–35 minutes, or until golden and hollow-sounding. Turn out on to a wire rack to cool.

Per stromboli Energy 2108kcal/8871kJ; Protein 96.5g; Carbohydrate 275.9g, of which sugars 9g; Fat 76.2g, of which saturates 41.7g; Cholesterol 177mg; Calcium 2125mg; Fibre 13.4g; Sodium 1536mg.
Per loaf Energy 2425kcal/10227kJ; Protein 105.4g; Carbohydrate 357.5g, of which sugars 21.6g; Fat 73.7g, of which saturates 40.8g; Cholesterol 364mg; Calcium 1978mg; Fibre 19.1g; Sodium 3826mg.

CHICKPEA AND PEPPERCORN BREAD

Bread may be a basic food, but it certainly isn't boring, as this exciting combination proves. Chickpeas help to keep the dough light, while pink and green peppercorns add colour and "explosions" of flavour.

SMALL

200ml/7fl oz/⅞ cup water
15ml/1 tbsp extra virgin olive oil
125g/4½oz/generous ⅔ cup canned chickpeas
375g/13oz/3¼ cups unbleached white bread flour
7.5ml/1½ tsp drained fresh pink peppercorns in brine
7.5ml/1½ tsp drained fresh green peppercorns in brine
15ml/1 tbsp skimmed milk powder (non fat dry milk)
5ml/1 tsp salt
7.5ml/1½ tsp granulated sugar
5ml/1 tsp easy bake (rapid-rise) dried yeast
milk, for brushing (optional)

MEDIUM

265ml/9½fl oz/1⅛ cup water
30ml/2 tbsp extra virgin olive oil
175g/6oz/1 cup canned chickpeas
500g/1lb 2oz/4½ cups unbleached white bread flour
10ml/2 tsp drained fresh pink peppercorns in brine
10ml/2 tsp drained fresh green peppercorns in brine
22ml/1½ tbsp skimmed milk powder
7.5ml/1½ tsp salt
10ml/2 tsp granulated sugar
7.5ml/1½ tsp easy bake dried yeast
milk, for brushing (optional)

LARGE

315ml/11fl oz/1⅛ cups water
45ml/3 tbsp extra virgin olive oil
200g/7oz/1 cup canned chickpeas
600g/1lb 5oz/5¼ cups unbleached white bread flour
10ml/2 tsp drained fresh pink peppercorns in brine
15ml/1 tbsp drained fresh green peppercorns in brine
30ml/2 tbsp skimmed milk powder
10ml/2 tsp salt
10ml/2 tsp granulated sugar
7.5ml/1½ tsp easy bake dried yeast
milk, for brushing (optional)

MAKES 1 LOAF

1 Pour the water and extra virgin olive oil into the bread machine pan. Add the well-drained chickpeas. If the instructions for your bread machine specify that the yeast is to be placed in the pan first, then simply reverse the order in which you add the liquid and dry ingredients to the bread pan.

2 Sprinkle over the flour, ensuring that it covers the ingredients already placed in the pan. Add the pink and green peppercorns and milk powder.

3 Place the salt and sugar in separate corners of the pan. Make a small indent in the centre of the flour (but not down as far as the liquid) and add the yeast.

4 Set the machine to white/basic. Select light crust, 500g for small; medium crust, large/750g for medium; or medium crust, 1kg/2lb for large. Press Start. Brush the top of the loaf with milk just before it starts to bake, if you like.

5 Remove the bread at the end of the baking cycle. Turn out on to a wire rack.

Per loaf Energy 1597kcal/6774kJ; Protein 47.6g; Carbohydrate 324.3g, of which sugars 19g; Fat 21.2g, of which saturates 3.7g; Cholesterol 6mg; Calcium 703mg; Fibre 16.8g; Sodium 2307mg.

GARLIC AND HERB WALNUT BREAD

Walnut bread is very popular in France. This variation includes both garlic and basil for additional flavour.

1 Pour the milk, water and olive oil into the bread machine pan. If the instructions for your machine specify that the yeast is to be placed in the pan first, reverse the order in which you add the liquid and dry ingredients.

2 Sprinkle over the flour and rolled oats, ensuring that they completely cover the liquid mixture. Add the chopped walnuts, garlic, oregano and basil. Place the salt and sugar in separate corners of the bread machine pan. Make a small indent in the centre of the flour (but do not go down as far as the liquid) and add the easy bake dried yeast.

3 Set the machine to white/basic, medium crust. Size: 500g for small, large/750g for medium or 1kg/2lb for large. Press Start.

4 Remove the bread at the end of the baking cycle and turn out on to a wire rack to cool.

SMALL
150ml/5fl oz/⅔ cup milk
60ml/2fl oz/4 tbsp water
30ml/2 tbsp extra virgin olive oil
325g/11½oz/scant 3 cups unbleached white bread flour
40g/1½oz/scant ⅓ cup rolled oats
40g/1½oz/⅓ cup chopped walnuts
1 garlic clove, finely chopped
5ml/1 tsp dried oregano
5ml/1 tsp chopped fresh basil
5ml/1 tsp salt
7.5ml/1½ tsp granulated sugar
2.5ml/½ tsp easy bake (rapid-rise) dried yeast

MEDIUM
185ml/6½fl oz/generous ¾ cup milk
105ml/7 tbsp water
45ml/3 tbsp extra virgin olive oil
450g/1lb/4 cups unbleached white bread flour
50g/2oz/½ cup rolled oats
50g/2oz/½ cup chopped walnuts
1½ garlic cloves, finely chopped
7.5ml/1½ tsp dried oregano
10ml/2 tsp chopped fresh basil
7.5ml/1½ tsp salt
10ml/2 tsp granulated sugar
5ml/1 tsp easy bake dried yeast

LARGE
180ml/6½fl oz/generous ¾ cup milk
130ml/4½fl oz/½ cup + 1 tbsp water
45ml/3 tbsp extra virgin olive oil
550g/1lb 4oz/5 cups unbleached white bread flour
65g/2½oz/generous ½ cup rolled oats
50g/2oz/½ cup chopped walnuts
2 garlic cloves, finely chopped
7.5ml/1½ tsp dried oregano
10ml/2 tsp chopped fresh basil
10ml/2 tsp salt
10ml/2 tsp granulated sugar
7.5ml/1½ tsp easy bake dried yeast

MAKES 1 LOAF

Per loaf Energy 1836kcal/7739kJ; Protein 46g; Carbohydrate 297.8g, of which sugars 20.8g; Fat 59.5g, of which saturates 7.4g; Cholesterol 8mg; Calcium 687mg; Fibre 14.2g; Sodium 2068mg.

SWEET POTATO BREAD

Adding sweet potato to the dough creates a loaf with a rich golden crust and the crumb is beautifully moist. Make sure you use the deep yellow sweet potatoes, in preference to the white variety of sweet potatoes, to give the bread a lovely colour.

SMALL
175g/6oz sweet potatoes, peeled
190ml/6¾fl oz/scant ⅞ cup water
350g/12oz/3 cups unbleached white bread flour
30ml/2 tbsp rolled oats
22ml/1½ tbsp skimmed milk powder (non fat dry milk)
5ml/1 tsp salt
15ml/1 tbsp muscovado (molasses) sugar
25g/1oz/2 tbsp butter
5ml/1 tsp easy bake (rapid-rise) dried yeast
FOR THE TOPPING
10ml/2 tsp water
5ml/1 tsp rolled oats
5ml/1 tsp wheat grain

MEDIUM
225g/8oz sweet potatoes, peeled
210ml/7½fl oz/scant 1 cup water
500g/1lb 2oz/4½ cups unbleached white bread flour
45ml/3 tbsp rolled oats
30ml/2 tbsp skimmed milk powder
7.5ml/1½ tsp salt
22ml/1½ tbsp muscovado sugar
40g/1½oz/3 tbsp butter
7.5ml/1½ tsp easy bake dried yeast
FOR THE TOPPING
15ml/1 tbsp water
10ml/2 tsp rolled oats
10ml/2 tsp wheat grain

LARGE
310g/11oz sweet potatoes, peeled
285ml/10fl oz/scant 1¼ cups water
600g/1lb 5oz/5¼ cups unbleached white bread flour
45ml/3 tbsp rolled oats
30ml/2 tbsp skimmed milk powder
7.5ml/1½ tsp salt
15ml/1 tbsp muscovado sugar
40g/1½oz/3 tbsp butter
7.5ml/1½ tsp easy bake dried yeast
FOR THE TOPPING
15ml/1 tbsp water
15ml/1 tbsp rolled oats
10ml/2 tsp wheat grain

MAKES 1 LOAF

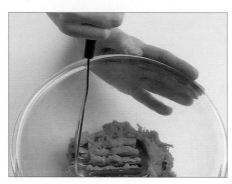

1 Cook the sweet potato in plenty of boiling water for 40 minutes or until very tender. Drain, and when cool enough to handle, peel off the skin. Place the sweet potato in a large bowl and mash well, but do not add any butter or milk.

2 Pour the water into the bread machine pan. However, if the instructions for your bread machine specify that the yeast is to be placed in the bread pan first, simply reverse the order in which you add the liquid and dry ingredients.

VARIATION
This bread is a good opportunity to use up any leftover sweet potato. If the potato has been mashed with milk and butter you may need to reduce the quantity of liquid a little. Use the following quantities of cooked, mashed sweet potatoes:
small machine: 125g/4½oz/1½ cups
medium machine: 175g/6oz/2 cups
large machine: 200g/7oz/2⅓ cups

COOK'S TIP
Rolled oats add a chewy texture and nutty taste to this loaf of bread. Make sure you use the traditional old-fashioned rolled oats, rather than "quick cook" oats.

3 Sprinkle the white bread flour, rolled oats and skimmed milk powder over the water, covering it completely. Weigh or measure the cooked sweet potatoes to ensure the quantity matches the amount given in the variation. Then add the potatoes to the bread pan.

4 Place the salt, sugar and butter in three separate corners of the bread machine pan. Make a shallow indent in the flour (but not down as far as the liquid underneath) and add the easy bake dried yeast.

5 Set the bread machine to the white/basic setting, medium crust. Size: 500g for small, large/750g for medium or 1kg/2lb for large. Press Start.

6 When the rising cycle is almost complete, just before the bread begins to bake, add the topping: brush the top of the loaf with the water and sprinkle the rolled oats and wheat grain over the top of the bread.

7 Remove the bread at the end of the baking cycle. Turn out on to a wire rack.

Per loaf Energy 1816kcal/7695kJ; Protein 44.1g; Carbohydrate 362.7g, of which sugars 35.9g; Fat 31.1g, of which saturates 15.4g; Cholesterol 63mg; Calcium 689mg; Fibre 18.1g; Sodium 2304mg.

SUN-DRIED TOMATO BREAD

The dense texture and highly concentrated flavour of sun-dried tomatoes makes them perfect for flavouring bread dough, and when Parmesan cheese is added, the result is an exceptionally tasty loaf.

SMALL

15g/½oz/¼ cup sun-dried tomatoes
130ml/4½fl oz/½ cup + 1 tbsp water
70ml/2½fl oz/¼ cup + 1 tbsp milk
15ml/1 tbsp extra virgin olive oil
325g/11½oz/scant 3 cups unbleached white bread flour
50g/2oz/½ cup wholemeal (whole-wheat) bread flour
40g/1½oz/½ cup freshly grated Parmesan cheese
5ml/1 tsp salt
5ml/1 tsp granulated sugar
4ml/¾ tsp easy bake (rapid-rise) dried yeast

MEDIUM

25g/1oz/½ cup sun-dried tomatoes
190ml/6¾fl oz/scant ⅞ cup water
115ml/4fl oz/½ cup milk
30ml/2 tbsp extra virgin olive oil
425g/15oz/3¾ cups unbleached white bread flour
75g/3oz/¾ cup wholemeal bread flour
50g/2oz/⅔ cup freshly grated Parmesan cheese
7.5ml/1½ tsp salt
10ml/2 tsp granulated sugar
5ml/1 tsp easy bake dried yeast

LARGE

35g/1⅓oz/¾ cup sun-dried tomatoes
210ml/7½fl oz/⅞ cup water
140ml/5fl oz/⅝ cup milk
30ml/2 tbsp extra virgin olive oil
500g/1lb 2oz/4½ cups unbleached white bread flour
100g/4oz/1 cup wholemeal bread flour
65g/2½oz/⅝ cup freshly grated Parmesan cheese
7.5ml/1½ tsp salt
10ml/2 tsp granulated sugar
7.5ml/1½ tsp easy bake dried yeast

MAKES 1 LOAF

1 Place the sun-dried tomatoes in a small bowl and pour over enough warm water to cover them. Leave to soak for 15 minutes, then tip into a sieve placed over a bowl. Allow to drain thoroughly, then chop finely.

2 Check the quantity of tomato water against the amount of water required for the loaf, and add more water if this is necessary. Pour it into the bread machine pan, then add the milk and olive oil. If the instructions for your machine specify that the yeast is to be placed in the pan first, then simply reverse the order in which you add the liquid and dry ingredients.

3 Sprinkle over both types of flour, ensuring that the liquid is completely covered. Sprinkle over the Parmesan, then add the salt and sugar, placing them in separate corners of the bread pan. Make a small indent in the centre of the flour (but not down as far as the liquid) and add the yeast.

4 Set the machine to white/basic; use the raisin setting (if available), medium crust. Size: 500g for small, large/750g for medium or 1kg/2lb for large. Press Start. Add the tomatoes when the machine beeps during the kneading cycle, or after the first kneading. Remove the bread at the end of the baking cycle. Turn on to a wire rack.

Per loaf Energy 1469kcal/6185kJ; Protein 31.2g; Carbohydrate 228.1g, of which sugars 23.6g; Fat 54.3g, of which saturates 9.1g; Cholesterol 9mg; Calcium 576mg; Fibre 8.8g; Sodium 1656mg.

POPPY SEED LOAF

Poppy seeds are popular in Eastern European breads. They have a mild, sweet, slightly nutty flavour and make an interesting addition to this loaf.

1 Pour the milk and water into the bread machine pan. If the instructions for your machine specify that the yeast is to be placed in the pan first, reverse the order in which you add the liquid and dry ingredients.

2 Sprinkle over the flour, ensuring that it covers the water. Then add the poppy seeds (see Cook's Tip).

3 Add the salt, sugar and butter in separate corners of the bread pan.

4 Make a small indent in the centre of the flour (but not down as far as the liquid) and add the yeast.

5 Set the machine to white/basic, medium crust. Size: 500g for small, large/750g for medium or 1kg/2lb for large. Press Start.

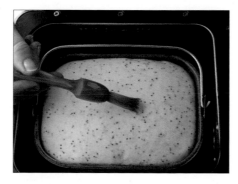

6 If glazing, mix the egg white and water and brush over the loaf just before the baking cycle starts.

SMALL
180ml/6½fl oz/generous ¾ cup milk
60ml/2fl oz/¼ cup water
375g/13oz/3¼ cups unbleached white
bread flour
45ml/3 tbsp poppy seeds
7.5ml/1½ tsp salt
10ml/2 tsp granulated sugar
20g/¾oz/1½ tbsp butter
5ml/1 tsp easy bake (rapid-rise)
dried yeast

MEDIUM
200ml/7fl oz/⅞ cup milk
100ml/3½fl oz/7 tbsp water
450g/1lb/4 cups unbleached white
bread flour
60ml/4 tbsp poppy seeds
7.5ml/1½ tsp salt
10ml/2 tsp granulated sugar
25g/1oz/2 tbsp butter
5ml/1 tsp easy bake dried yeast

LARGE
265ml/9½fl oz/1⅛ cup milk
120ml/generous 4fl oz/½ cup water
625g/1lb 6oz/5½ cups unbleached
white bread flour
60ml/4 tbsp poppy seeds
10ml/2 tsp salt
15ml/1 tbsp granulated sugar
25g/1oz/2 tbsp butter
7.5ml/1½ tsp easy bake dried yeast

FOR THE GLAZE (OPTIONAL)
½ egg white
5ml/1 tsp water

MAKES 1 LOAF

7 Remove the bread at the end of the baking cycle and turn out on to a wire rack to cool.

COOK'S TIP
If you want to ensure the poppy seeds stay whole, do not add them at the start, but add them when the machine beeps, or during the last 5 minutes of kneading.

Per loaf Energy 1817kcal/7674kJ; Protein 49.5g; Carbohydrate 311.2g, of which sugars 25.3g; Fat 50.4g, of which saturates 17.1g; Cholesterol 57mg; Calcium 1052mg; Fibre 15.2g; Sodium 3217mg.

GRAINY MUSTARD AND BEER LOAF

For a ploughman's lunch par excellence, serve chunks of this wonderful bread with cheese and pickles.

SMALL
210ml/7½fl oz/scant 1 cup flat beer
15ml/1 tbsp vegetable oil
30ml/2 tbsp wholegrain mustard
250g/9oz/2¼ cups unbleached white
bread flour
125g/4½oz/generous 1 cup wholemeal
(whole-wheat) bread flour
15ml/1 tbsp skimmed milk powder
(non fat dry milk)
5ml/1 tsp salt
7.5ml/1½ tsp granulated sugar
5ml/1 tsp easy bake (rapid-rise)
dried yeast

MEDIUM
280ml/10fl oz/1¼ cups flat beer
15ml/1 tbsp vegetable oil
45ml/3 tbsp wholegrain mustard
350g/12oz/3 cups unbleached white
bread flour
150g/5½oz/1⅓ cups wholemeal
bread flour
22ml/1½ tbsp skimmed milk powder
7.5ml/1½ tsp salt
10ml/2 tsp granulated sugar
5ml/1 tsp easy bake dried yeast

LARGE
330ml/scant 12fl oz/1¼ cups + 2 tbsp
flat beer
30ml/2 tbsp vegetable oil
45ml/3 tbsp wholegrain mustard
425g/15oz/3¾ cups unbleached white
bread flour
175g/6oz/generous 1½ cups
wholemeal bread flour
30ml/2 tbsp skimmed milk powder
7.5ml/1½ tsp salt
15ml/1 tbsp granulated sugar
7.5ml/1½ tsp easy bake dried yeast

MAKES 1 LOAF

COOK'S TIP
Use pale ale for a more subtle taste or brown ale if you prefer a stronger flavour to your bread. Open the beer at least 1 hour before using, to make sure it is flat.

1 Pour the beer and oil into the bread machine pan. Add the mustard. If the instructions for your machine specify that the yeast is to be placed in the pan first, reverse the order in which you add the liquid and dry ingredients.

2 Sprinkle over the white and wholemeal flours, ensuring that the liquid is completely covered. Add the skimmed milk powder. Add the salt and sugar, placing them in separate corners of the bread pan. Make a small indent in the centre of the flour (but not down as far as the liquid) and add the yeast.

3 Set the bread machine to the white/basic setting, medium crust. Size: 500g for small, large/750g for medium or 1kg/2lb for large. Press Start.

4 Remove the bread at the end of the baking cycle and turn out on to a wire rack to cool.

Per loaf Energy 1522kcal/6447kJ; Protein 45.8g; Carbohydrate 293.1g, of which sugars 25.2g; Fat 21.7g, of which saturates 3.2g; Cholesterol 6mg; Calcium 574mg; Fibre 20.5g; Sodium 570mg.

GOLDEN PUMPKIN BREAD

*The pumpkin purée gives this loaf a rich golden crumb, a soft crust and a
beautifully moist light texture, as well as a delightfully sweet-savoury flavour.
It is worth noting that corn meal is sometimes known as maize meal.*

1 Mash the pumpkin and put it in the
bread machine pan. Add the buttermilk,
water and oil. If the instructions for your
machine specify that the easy bake
dried yeast is to be placed in the pan
first, reverse the order in which you add
the liquid mixture and dry ingredients.

2 Sprinkle over the flour and corn meal,
ensuring that the liquid is completely
covered. Add the golden syrup and salt
in separate corners of the bread
machine pan. Make an indent in the
centre of the flour (but not down as far
as the liquid) and add the yeast.

SMALL
150g/5½oz cooked pumpkin, cooled
90ml/6 tbsp buttermilk
60ml/4 tbsp water
15ml/1 tbsp extra virgin olive oil
325g/11½oz/scant 3 cups unbleached
white bread flour
50g/2oz/½ cup corn meal
15ml/1 tbsp golden (light corn) syrup
5ml/1 tsp salt
4ml/¾ tsp easy bake (rapid-rise)
dried yeast
15ml/1 tbsp pumpkin seeds

MEDIUM
200g/7oz cooked pumpkin, cooled
110ml/scant 4fl oz/scant ½ cup
buttermilk
45ml/3 tbsp water
30ml/2 tbsp extra virgin olive oil
425g/15oz/3¾ cups unbleached white
bread flour
75g/3oz/¾ cup corn meal
22ml/1½ tbsp golden syrup
7.5ml/1½ tsp salt
5ml/1 tsp easy bake dried yeast
22ml/1½ tbsp pumpkin seeds

LARGE
225g/8oz cooked pumpkin, cooled
140ml/5fl oz/⅝ cup buttermilk
70ml/2½fl oz/scant ⅓ cup water
45ml/3 tbsp extra virgin olive oil
525g/1lb 3oz/4¾ cups unbleached
white bread flour
75g/3oz/⅔ cup corn meal
30ml/2 tbsp golden syrup
10ml/2 tsp salt
7.5ml/1½ tsp easy bake dried yeast
30ml/2 tbsp pumpkin seeds

MAKES 1 LOAF

3 Set the machine to white/basic, raisin
setting (if available), medium crust. Size:
500g for small, large/750g for medium or
1kg/2lb for large. Add the pumpkin seeds
to the automatic dispenser, if available (if
adding manually, add when the machine
beeps during the kneading cycle). Press
Start. Remove at the end of the baking
cycle. Turn out on to a wire rack to cool.

Per loaf Energy 1527kcal/6461kJ; Protein 42.1g; Carbohydrate 299.5g, of which sugars 12.3g; Fat 24.7g, of which saturates 3.1g; Cholesterol 3mg; Calcium 616mg; Fibre 13.7g; Sodium 2138mg.

MIXED HERB COTTAGE LOAF

300ml/10½fl oz/1¼ cups water
450g/1lb/4 cups unbleached white
bread flour, plus extra for dusting
7.5ml/1½ tsp granulated sugar
7.5ml/1½ tsp salt
7.5ml/1½ tsp easy bake (rapid-rise)
dried yeast
15ml/1 tbsp chopped fresh chives
10ml/2 tsp chopped fresh thyme
15ml/1 tbsp chopped fresh tarragon
30ml/2 tbsp chopped fresh parsley
5ml/1 tsp salt, to glaze
15ml/1 tbsp water, to glaze

MAKES 1 LOAF

There's something very satisfying about the shape of a cottage loaf, and the flavour of fresh herbs – chives, thyme, tarragon and parsley – adds to the appeal. This loaf makes the perfect centrepiece for the table, for guests to help themselves.

1 Pour the water into the bread machine pan. If the operating instructions for your bread machine specify that the yeast is to be placed in the pan first, then simply reverse the order in which you add the water and dry ingredients.

2 Sprinkle over the flour, ensuring that it covers the water completely. Add the granulated sugar and the salt, placing them in separate corners of the bread machine pan. Make a small indent in the centre of the flour (but do not go down as far as the water) and add the easy bake dried yeast.

3 Set the bread machine to the dough setting; use basic raisin dough setting (if available). Press Start.

4 Add the chives, thyme, tarragon and parsley when the machine beeps to add extra ingredients, or during the final 5 minutes of kneading. Lightly flour two baking sheets.

5 When the dough cycle has finished, remove the dough from the machine. Place it on a surface that has been lightly floured. Knock the dough back (punch it down) gently and then divide it into two pieces, making one piece twice as large as the other.

6 Take each piece of dough in turn and shape it into a plump ball. Place the balls of dough on the prepared baking sheets and cover each with a lightly oiled mixing bowl.

7 Leave in a warm place for about 20–30 minutes, or until the dough has almost doubled in size.

8 Cut a cross, about 4cm/1½in across, in the top of the larger piece of dough. Brush the surface with water and place the smaller round on top.

9 Carefully press the handle of a wooden spoon through the centre of both pieces of dough. Cover the loaf with oiled clear film (plastic wrap) and leave it to rise for 10 minutes.

10 Meanwhile, preheat the oven to 220°C/425°F/Gas 7. Mix the salt and water for the glaze in a bowl, then brush the mixture over the top of the bread.

11 Using a sharp knife, make eight long slashes around the top of the bread and 12 small slashes around the base. Dust the top of the bread lightly with white bread flour.

12 Bake for 30–35 minutes, or until the bread is golden and sounds hollow when tapped on the base. Turn the loaf out on to a wire rack to cool.

VARIATION
Vary the combination of fresh herbs you use, according to availability and taste. You should aim for just under 75ml/5 tbsp in all, but use more pungent herbs sparingly, so they do not become too overpowering.

Per loaf Energy 1581kcal/6722kJ; Protein 43.8g; Carbohydrate 358.8g, of which sugars 15.7g; Fat 6.5g, of which saturates 0.9g; Cholesterol 0mg; Calcium 734mg; Fibre 16.4g; Sodium 1995mg.

VENISON TORDU

This pretty twisted bread is punctuated with strips of smoked venison, black pepper and crushed juniper berries. It tastes delicious on its own, perhaps with a glass of red wine. Alternatively, cut the bread into thick slices and serve it with olives and nuts as a precursor to an Italian meal.

230ml/8fl oz/1 cup water
350g/12oz/3 cups unbleached white bread flour
5ml/1 tsp granulated sugar
5ml/1 tsp salt
5ml/1 tsp easy bake (rapid-rise) dried yeast
40g/1½oz smoked venison, cut into strips
5ml/1 tsp freshly ground black pepper
5ml/1 tsp juniper berries, crushed
unbleached white bread flour, for dusting

MAKES 1 LOAF

1 Pour the water into the bread machine pan. If the instructions for your bread machine specify that the yeast is to be placed in the pan first, simply reverse the order in which you add the liquid and dry ingredients to the pan.

2 Sprinkle over the white bread flour, ensuring that it completely covers the water. Add the sugar and salt, placing them in separate corners of the bread pan. Make a shallow indent in the centre of the flour (but not down as far as the liquid) and add the easy bake dried yeast.

3 Set the bread machine to the dough setting; use basic dough setting (if available). Press Start. Meanwhile, lightly oil a baking sheet.

4 When the dough cycle has finished, remove the dough from the bread machine pan and place it on a lightly floured surface. Knock it back (punch it down) gently. Shape the dough into a ball and flatten the top slightly.

5 Roll the dough out to a round, about 2cm/¾in thick. Sprinkle the top of the dough with venison strips, black pepper and juniper berries. Leave a 1cm/½in clear border around the edge.

6 Fold one side of the dough to the centre, then repeat on the other side.

7 Press the folds gently with a rolling pin to seal them, then fold again along the centre line.

COOK'S TIP
Try using cured and smoked venison, marinated in olive oil and herbs, for this recipe. The olive oil and herbs add an extra flavour which beautifully complements this bread. Alternatively, sprinkle 5ml/1 tsp of dried herbs such as rosemary, thyme, sage or oregano over the dough in step 4.

8 Press the seam gently to seal, then roll the dough backwards and forwards to make a loaf about 65cm/26in long.

9 Using the side of your hand, press across the centre of the loaf to make an indentation. Bring both ends towards each other to make an upside down "U" shape and twist together.

10 Place the venison tordu on the prepared baking sheet. Cover the loaf with lightly oiled clear film (plastic wrap) and leave to rise in a warm place for 30 minutes, or until it has almost doubled in size. Meanwhile, preheat the oven to 220°C/425°F/Gas 7. Remove the clear film and dust the top of the twisted loaf with white bread flour.

11 Bake for 25–30 minutes, or until the bread is golden and sounds hollow when tapped on the base. Turn out on to a wire rack to cool. Serve freshly baked, while the bread is still slightly warm.

Per loaf Energy 1265kcal/5377kJ; Protein 42.5g; Carbohydrate 277.9g, of which sugars 9.4g; Fat 6.1g, of which saturates 1.1g; Cholesterol 20mg; Calcium 504mg; Fibre 10.9g; Sodium 1999mg.

ROLLS, BUNS AND PASTRIES

These hand-shaped delights include French Petit Pain au Chocolat, Italian Ricotta and Oregano Knots, and Apple and Sultana Danish Pastries. Chelsea Buns and Wholemeal Muffins are British classics, while Breakfast Pancakes and Doughnuts are traditional American offerings. Sweet and savoury rolls using mixed grains, herbs, nuts and fruit are just a few of the characterful small breads to enjoy in this section.

50g/2oz/generous ⅓ cup pudding rice
280ml/10fl oz/1¼ cups milk
140ml/5fl oz/⅝ cup water
2 eggs
125g/4½oz/generous 1 cup
unbleached white bread flour
5ml/1 tsp grated lemon rind
2.5ml/½ tsp ground ginger
2.5ml/½ tsp freshly grated nutmeg
50g/2oz/¼ cup caster (superfine) sugar
1.5ml/¼ tsp salt
5ml/1 tsp easy bake (rapid-rise)
dried yeast
oil, for deep-frying
icing (confectioners') sugar, for dusting

MAKES ABOUT 25

1 Place the rice, milk and water in a pan and slowly bring to the boil. Lower the heat, cover and simmer for 20 minutes, stirring occasionally, until the rice is soft and the liquid absorbed. Leave to cool.

2 Add the eggs to the bread machine pan. Reverse the order in which you add the wet and dry ingredients if necessary.

CALAS

These tasty morsels are a Creole speciality, made from a rice-based yeast dough which is then deep-fried. They are delicious served warm with coffee or as a breakfast treat.

3 Add the rice. Sprinkle over the flour, then the lemon rind, ginger and nutmeg. Add the sugar and salt, placing them in separate corners of the bread pan. Make a small indent in the centre of the flour (but not down as far as the liquid) and add the yeast.

4 Set the bread machine to the dough setting; use basic dough setting (if available). Press Start. When the dough cycle has finished, lift out the pan containing the batter from the machine.

5 Preheat the oven to 140°C/275°F/ Gas 1. Heat the oil for deep-frying to 180°C/350°F or until a cube of dried bread, added to the oil, turns golden in 45 seconds. Add tablespoons of batter a few at a time and fry for 3–4 minutes, turning occasionally, until golden.

6 Use a slotted spoon to remove the calas from the oil and drain on kitchen paper. Keep them warm in the oven while you cook the remainder. When all the calas have been cooked, dust them with icing sugar and serve warm.

> **COOK'S TIP**
> If you are using a large bread machine it is a good idea to make double the quantity of dough. If you use the quantities listed here, it is important to check that all the flour is thoroughly mixed with the liquid.

---

2 eggs
280ml/10fl oz/1¼ cups milk
225g/8oz/2 cups unbleached white bread flour
5ml/1 tsp salt
15ml/1 tbsp caster (superfine) sugar
15g/½oz/1 tbsp butter, melted
5ml/1 tsp easy bake (rapid-rise) dried yeast
maple syrup or wild cranberry sauce, to serve

MAKES ABOUT 15

1 Separate 1 egg and set the white aside. Place the yolk in the machine pan and add the whole egg and the milk. If the instructions for your machine specify that the yeast is to be placed in the pan first, reverse the order in which you add the liquid and dry ingredients.

AMERICAN BREAKFAST PANCAKES

These thick, succulent breakfast pancakes are often served with a sauce made from wild cranberries, also known as lingonberries. They are equally delicious served with maple syrup and with strips of crispy bacon.

2 Sprinkle over the flour, ensuring that it covers the liquid. Add the salt, sugar and butter, placing them in separate corners of the bread pan. Make a small indent in the centre of the flour (but not down as far as the liquid) and add the easy bake dried yeast.

3 Set the bread machine to the dough setting; use basic dough setting (if available). Press Start.

4 When the dough cycle has finished pour the batter into a large measuring jug. Whisk the reserved egg white; fold it into the batter. Preheat the oven to 140°C/275°F/Gas 1.

5 Lightly oil a large heavy frying pan or griddle and place over a medium heat. Add about 45ml/3 tbsp batter, letting it spread out to form a pancake about 10cm/4in wide. If room, make a second pancake alongside the first.

6 Cook each pancake until the surface begins to dry out, then turn over using a fish slice or spatula and cook the other side for about 1 minute, or until golden.

7 Stack the pancakes between sheets of baking parchment on a warm plate and keep them warm in the oven while you cook the rest of the batter. Serve the pancakes with the syrup or sauce.

Per cala Energy 80kcal/335kJ; Protein 1.6g; Carbohydrate 8.3g, of which sugars 2.7g; Fat 4.8g, of which saturates 0.7g; Cholesterol 16mg; Calcium 25mg; Fibre 0.2g; Sodium 12mg.
Per pancake Energy 81kcal/342kJ; Protein 2.9g; Carbohydrate 13.6g, of which sugars 2.2g; Fat 2.1g, of which saturates 1g; Cholesterol 29mg; Calcium 48mg; Fibre 0.5g; Sodium 159mg.

PETITS PAINS AU CHOCOLAT

*A freshly baked petit pain au chocolat is almost impossible to resist, with its
buttery, flaky yet crisp pastry concealing a delectable chocolate filling.
For a special finish, drizzle melted chocolate over the tops of the
freshly baked and cooked pastries.*

125ml/4½fl oz/generous ½ cup water
*250g/9oz/2¼ cups unbleached white
bread flour*
*30ml/2 tbsp skimmed milk powder
(non fat dry milk)*
15ml/1 tbsp caster (superfine) sugar
2.5ml/½ tsp salt
140g/5oz/⅔ cup butter, softened
*7.5ml/1½ tsp easy bake (rapid-rise)
dried yeast*
*225g/8oz plain (semisweet) chocolate,
broken into pieces*

FOR THE GLAZE
1 egg yolk
15ml/1 tbsp milk

MAKES 9

1 Pour the water into the machine pan.
If the instructions for your machine
specify that the yeast is to be placed in
the pan first, then reverse the order in
which you add liquid and dry ingredients.

2 Sprinkle over the flour, then the
skimmed milk powder, ensuring that the
water is completely covered.

3 Add the caster sugar, salt and 25g/1oz/
2 tbsp of the softened butter, placing
them in separate corners of the bread
pan. Make a small indent in the centre
of the flour (but not down as far as the
liquid) and add the yeast.

4 Set the breadmaking machine to the
dough setting; use basic dough setting
(if available). Press Start. Meanwhile
shape the remaining softened butter
into an oblong-shaped block, about
2cm/¾in thick.

5 Lightly grease two baking sheets. When
the dough cycle has finished, place the
dough on a floured surface. Knock back
(punch down) and shape into a ball. Cut a
cross halfway through the top of the dough.

6 Roll out around the cross, leaving a
risen centre. Place the butter in the
centre. Fold the rolled dough over the
butter to enclose; seal the edges.

7 Roll to a rectangle 2cm/¾in thick,
twice as long as wide. Fold the bottom
third up and the top down; seal the
edges with a rolling pin. Wrap in lightly
oiled clear film (plastic wrap). Place in
the refrigerator and chill for 20 minutes.

8 Do the same again twice more, giving
a quarter turn and chilling each time.
Chill again for 30 minutes.

9 Roll out the dough to a rectangle
measuring 52 × 30cm/21 × 12in. Using a
sharp knife, cut the dough into three
strips lengthways and widthways to
make nine 18 × 10cm/7 × 4in rectangles.

10 Divide the chocolate among the
nine dough rectangles, placing the
pieces lengthways at one short end.

11 Mix the egg yolk and milk for the
glaze together. Brush the mixture over
the edges of the dough.

12 Roll up each piece of dough to
completely enclose the chocolate,
then press the edges together to seal.

13 Place the pastries seam side down on
the prepared baking sheets. Cover with
oiled clear film and leave to rise in a
warm place for about 30 minutes or
until doubled in size.

14 Meanwhile, preheat the oven to
200°C/400°F/Gas 6. Brush the pastries
with the remaining glaze and bake for
about 15 minutes, or until golden. Turn
out on to a wire rack to cool just slightly
and serve warm.

VARIATION
Fill this flaky yeast pastry with a
variety of sweet and savoury fillings.
Try chopped nuts, tossed with a little
brown sugar and cinnamon or, for a
savoury filling, thin strips of cheese,
wrapped in ham or mixed with
chopped cooked bacon.

Per pain au chocolat Energy 352kcal/1473kJ; Protein 4.2g; Carbohydrate 40.1g, of which sugars 17.6g; Fat 20.6g, of which saturates 12.8g; Cholesterol 39mg; Calcium 65mg; Fibre 0.9g; Sodium 126mg.

WHOLEMEAL ENGLISH MUFFINS

After a long walk on a wintry afternoon, come home to warm muffins,
carefully torn apart and spread thickly with butter.

350ml/12fl oz/1½ cups milk
225g/8oz/2 cups unbleached white
bread flour
225g/8oz/2 cups stoneground
wholemeal (whole-wheat) bread flour
5ml/1 tsp caster (superfine) sugar
7.5ml/1½ tsp salt
15g/½oz/1 tbsp butter
7.5ml/1½ tsp easy bake (rapid-rise)
dried yeast
rice flour or fine semolina, for dusting

MAKES 9

COOK'S TIP
If you don't have a griddle, cook the
muffins in a heavy frying pan. It is
important that they cook slowly.

1 Pour the milk into the bread machine
pan. If the instructions for your bread
machine specify that the yeast is to be
placed in the pan first, then reverse the
order in which you add the liquid and
dry ingredients.

2 Sprinkle over each type of flour in
turn, making sure that the milk is
completely covered. Add the caster
sugar, salt and butter, placing each of
them in separate corners of the bread
pan. Then make a small indent in the
centre of the flour (but do not go down
as far as the liquid underneath) and add
the easy bake dried yeast.

3 Set the machine to the dough setting;
use basic dough setting (if available).
Press Start. Sprinkle a baking sheet
with rice flour or semolina.

4 When the dough cycle has finished, place
the dough on a floured surface. Knock it
back (punch it down) gently. Roll out
the dough until it is about 1cm/½in thick.

5 Using a floured 7.5cm/3in plain cutter,
cut out nine muffins. If you like, you can
re-roll the trimmings, knead them
together and let the dough rest for a few
minutes before rolling it out again and
cutting out an extra muffin or two.

6 Place the muffins on the baking sheet.
Dust with rice flour or semolina. Cover
with oiled clear film (plastic wrap) and
leave in a warm place for 20 minutes, or
until almost doubled in size.

7 Heat a griddle over a medium heat.
You should not need any oil if the
griddle is well seasoned; if not, add the
merest trace of oil. Cook the muffins
slowly, three at a time, for about
7 minutes on each side. Serve warm.

Per muffin Energy 235kcal/997kJ; Protein 7.4g; Carbohydrate 48.2g, of which sugars 3.2g; Fat 2.8g, of which saturates 0.7g; Cholesterol 2mg; Calcium 121mg; Fibre 2.5g; Sodium 351mg.

HOT CROSS BUNS

The traditional cross on these Easter buns originates from early civilization and probably symbolized the four seasons; it was only later used to mark Good Friday and the Crucifixion.

210ml/7½fl oz/scant 1 cup milk
1 egg
450g/1lb/4 cups unbleached white bread flour
7.5ml/1½ tsp mixed (apple pie) spice
2.5ml/½ tsp ground cinnamon
2.5ml/½ tsp salt
50g/2oz/¼ cup caster (superfine) sugar
50g/2oz/¼ cup butter
7.5ml/1½ tsp easy bake (rapid-rise) dried yeast
75g/3oz/scant ½ cup currants
25g/1oz/3 tbsp sultanas (golden raisins)
25g/1oz/3 tbsp cut mixed (candied) peel

FOR THE PASTRY CROSSES
50g/2oz/½ cup plain (all-purpose) flour
25g/1oz/2 tbsp margarine

FOR THE GLAZE
30ml/2 tbsp milk
25g/1oz/2 tbsp caster sugar

MAKES 12

COOK'S TIP
If you prefer, to make the crosses roll out 50g/2oz shortcrust (unsweetened) pastry, and cut into narrow strips. Brush the buns with water to attach the crosses.

1 Pour the milk and egg into the bread pan. Reverse the order in which you add the liquid and dry ingredients if your machine requires this.

2 Sprinkle over the flour, ensuring that it covers the liquid. Add the mixed spice and cinnamon. Place the salt, sugar and butter in separate corners of the pan. Make a shallow indent in the centre of the flour and add the yeast.

3 Set the bread machine to the dough setting; use basic raisin dough setting (if available). Press Start. Lightly grease two baking sheets.

4 Add the currants, sultanas and mixed peel when the machine beeps or 5 minutes before the end of the kneading period.

5 When the dough cycle has finished, remove the dough from the machine and place it on a lightly floured surface. Knock it back (punch it down) gently, then divide it into 12 pieces. Cup each piece between your hands and shape it into a ball. Place on the prepared baking sheets, cover with oiled clear film (plastic wrap) and leave for 30–45 minutes or until almost doubled in size.

6 Meanwhile, preheat the oven to 200°C/400°F/Gas 6. Make the pastry for the crosses. In a bowl, rub the flour and margarine together until the mixture resembles fine breadcrumbs. Bind with enough water to make a soft pastry which can be piped.

7 Spoon the pastry into a piping bag fitted with a plain nozzle and pipe a cross on each bun. Bake the buns for 15–18 minutes, or until golden.

8 Meanwhile, heat the milk and sugar for the glaze in a small pan. Stir thoroughly until the sugar dissolves. Brush the glaze over the top of the hot buns. Turn out on to a wire rack. Serve warm or cool.

Per bun Energy 155kcal/657kJ; Protein 3.7g; Carbohydrate 29.3g, of which sugars 11.7g; Fat 3.4g, of which saturates 1.1g; Cholesterol 16mg; Calcium 55mg; Fibre 0.9g; Sodium 60mg.

RICOTTA AND OREGANO KNOTS

The ricotta cheese adds a wonderful moistness to these beautifully shaped rolls. Serve them slightly warm to appreciate fully the flavour of the oregano as your butter melts into the crumb.

60ml/4 tbsp ricotta cheese
225ml/8fl oz/scant 1 cup water
450g/1lb/4 cups unbleached white
bread flour
45ml/3 tbsp skimmed milk powder
(non fat dry milk)
10ml/2 tsp dried oregano
5ml/1 tsp salt
10ml/2 tsp caster (superfine) sugar
25g/1oz/ 2 tbsp butter
5ml/1 tsp easy bake (rapid-rise)
dried yeast

FOR THE TOPPING
1 egg yolk
freshly ground black pepper

MAKES 12

1 Spoon the cheese into the bread machine pan and add the water. Reverse the order in which you add the liquid and dry ingredients if necessary.

2 Sprinkle over the flour, ensuring that it covers the cheese and water. Add the skimmed milk powder and oregano. Place the salt, sugar and butter in separate corners of the bread pan. Make a small indent in the centre of the flour (but not down as far as the liquid) and add the yeast.

3 Set the bread machine to the dough setting; use basic dough setting (if available). Press Start. Lightly oil two baking sheets.

4 When the dough cycle has finished, remove the dough from the machine and place it on a lightly floured surface.

5 Knock the dough back (punch it down) gently, then divide it into 12 pieces and cover with oiled clear film (plastic wrap).

6 Take one piece of dough, leaving the rest covered, and roll it on the floured surface into a rope about 25cm/10in long. Lift one end of the dough over the other to make a loop. Push the end through the hole in the loop to make a neat knot.

7 Repeat with the remaining dough. Place the knots on the prepared baking sheets, cover them with oiled clear film and leave to rise in a warm place for about 30 minutes, or until doubled in size. Meanwhile, preheat the oven to 220°C/425°F/Gas 7.

8 Mix the egg yolk and 15ml/1tbsp water for the topping in a small bowl. Brush the mixture over the rolls. Sprinkle some with freshly ground black pepper and leave the rest plain.

9 Bake for about 15–18 minutes, or until the rolls are golden brown. Turn out on to a wire rack to cool.

Per knot Energy 160kcal/678kJ; Protein 4.3g; Carbohydrate 30.7g, of which sugars 2.1g; Fat 3.1g, of which saturates 1.8g; Cholesterol 7mg; Calcium 65mg; Fibre 1.2g; Sodium 186mg.

WHOLEMEAL AND RYE PISTOLETS

A wholemeal and rye version of this French and Belgian speciality. Unless your bread machine has a programme for wholewheat dough, it is worth the extra effort of the double rising, because this gives a lighter roll with a more developed flavour.

290ml/10¼fl oz/1¼ cups water
280g/10oz/2½ cups stoneground wholemeal (whole-wheat) bread flour
50g/2oz/½ cup unbleached white bread flour, plus extra for dusting
115g/4oz/1 cup rye flour
30ml/2 tbsp skimmed milk powder (non fat dry milk)
10ml/2 tsp salt + 5ml/1tsp to glaze
10ml/2 tsp caster (superfine) sugar
25g/1oz/2 tbsp butter
7.5ml/1½ tsp easy bake (rapid-rise) dried yeast

MAKES 12

5 Leaving the rest of the dough covered, shape one piece into a ball. Roll on the floured surface into an oval. Repeat with the remaining dough.

6 Place the rolls on the prepared baking sheets. Cover them with oiled clear film and leave them in a warm place for about 30–45 minutes, or until almost doubled in size. Meanwhile preheat the oven to 220°C/425°F/Gas 7.

7 Mix the salt with 15ml/1tbsp water for the glaze and brush over the rolls. Dust the tops of the rolls with flour.

1 Pour the water into the bread pan. If the instructions for your machine specify that the yeast is to be placed in the pan first, reverse the order in which you add the liquid and dry ingredients.

2 Sprinkle over all three types of flour, ensuring that the water is completely covered. Add the skimmed milk powder. Then add the salt, sugar and butter, placing them in separate corners of the bread pan. Make a small indent in the centre of the flour (but do not go down as far as the water underneath) and add the easy bake dried yeast.

3 Set the bread machine to the dough setting; use wholewheat dough setting (if available). If you have only one basic dough setting you may need to repeat the programme to allow sufficient time for this heavier dough to rise. Press Start. Lightly oil two baking sheets.

4 When the dough cycle has finished, remove the dough from the bread machine pan and place it on a surface that has been lightly floured. Knock the dough back (punch it down) gently, then divide it into 12 pieces. Cover with oiled clear film (plastic wrap).

8 Using the oiled handle of a wooden spoon held horizontally, split each roll almost in half, along its length. Replace the clear film and leave for 10 minutes.

9 Bake the rolls for 15–20 minutes, until the bases sound hollow when tapped. Turn out on to a wire rack to cool.

Per pistolet Energy 142kcal/601kJ; Protein 4.5g; Carbohydrate 26.8g, of which sugars 1.9g; Fat 2.6g, of which saturates 1.3g; Cholesterol 5mg; Calcium 31mg; Fibre 3.4g; Sodium 186mg.

DOUGHNUTS

The main thing to remember about doughnuts is the speed with which they disappear, so make plenty of both the cinnamon-coated rings and the round ones filled with jam.

90ml/6 tbsp water
140ml/5fl oz/scant ⅔ cup milk
1 egg
450g/1lb/4 cups unbleached white bread flour
50g/2oz/¼ cup caster (superfine) sugar
5ml/1 tsp salt
50g/2oz/¼ cup butter
7.5ml/1½ tsp easy bake (rapid-rise) dried yeast
oil for deep-frying
caster (superfine) sugar, for sprinkling
ground cinnamon, for sprinkling

FOR THE FILLING
45ml/3 tbsp red jam
5ml/1 tsp lemon juice

MAKES ABOUT 16

1 Pour the water and milk into the bread machine pan. Break in the egg. If the instructions for your bread machine specify that the yeast is to be placed in the pan first, simply reverse the order in which you add the liquid and dry ingredients.

2 Sprinkle over the flour, ensuring that it covers the liquid. Add the sugar, salt and butter, placing them in separate corners of the bread pan. Make a small indent in the centre of the flour (but not down as far as the liquid) and add the easy bake dried yeast.

3 Set the bread machine to the dough setting; use basic dough setting (if available). Press Start.

4 When the dough cycle has finished, remove the dough from the machine and place it on a lightly floured surface.

5 Knock the dough back (punch it down) gently and divide it in half. Cover one half with lightly oiled clear film (plastic wrap). Divide the remaining piece into eight equal portions.

6 Take each portion in turn and use your hands to roll it into a smooth ball. Lightly oil two baking sheets.

7 Place the eight dough balls on one of the prepared baking sheets. Cover them with oiled clear film and leave in a warm place to rise for about 30 minutes, or until doubled in size.

8 Roll the remaining dough out to a thickness of 1cm/½in. Cut into circles using a 7.5cm/3in plain cutter. Then make the dough circles into rings using a 4cm/1½in plain cutter.

9 Place the rings on the remaining baking sheet, cover them with oiled clear film and leave them in a warm place for about 30 minutes, or until doubled in size.

10 Heat the oil for deep-frying to 180°C/350°F, or until a cube of dried bread, added to the oil, turns golden brown in 30–60 seconds. Add the doughnuts, three or four at a time.

11 Cook the doughnuts for about 4–5 minutes, or until they are golden. Remove from the oil using a slotted spoon and drain on kitchen paper.

12 Toss the round doughnuts in caster sugar and the ring doughnuts in a mixture of caster sugar and ground cinnamon. Set aside to cool.

13 Heat the jam and lemon juice in a small pan until warm, stirring to combine. Leave to cool, then spoon the mixture into a piping (pastry) bag fitted with a small plain nozzle.

14 When the round doughnuts have cooled, use a skewer to make a small hole in each. Insert the piping nozzle and squeeze a little of the jam mixture into each doughnut.

Per doughnut Energy 192kcal/802kJ; Protein 2.5g; Carbohydrate 22.6g, of which sugars 8.3g; Fat 10.8g, of which saturates 1.4g; Cholesterol 16mg; Calcium 37mg; Fibre 0.6g; Sodium 11mg.

CHELSEA BUNS

Chelsea buns are said to have been invented by the owner of the Chelsea Bun House in London at the end of the 17th century. They make the perfect accompaniment to a cup of coffee or tea. They are so delicious, it is difficult to resist going back for more!

225ml/8fl oz/scant 1 cup milk
1 egg
500g/1lb 2oz/4½ cups unbleached white bread flour
2.5ml/½ tsp salt
75g/3oz/6 tbsp caster (superfine) sugar
50g/2oz/¼ cup butter, softened
5ml/1 tsp easy bake (rapid-rise) dried yeast
50g/2oz/¼ cup caster (superfine) sugar, to glaze
5ml/1 tsp orange flower water, to glaze

For the Filling
25g/1oz/2 tbsp butter, melted
115g/4oz/⅔ cup sultanas (golden raisins)
25g/1oz/3 tbsp mixed chopped (candied) peel
25g/1oz/2 tbsp currants
25g/1oz/2 tbsp soft light brown sugar
5ml/1 tsp mixed (apple pie) spice

Makes 12 Buns

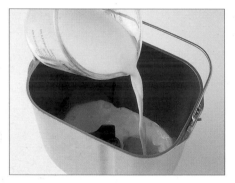

1 Pour the milk into the bread machine pan. Add the egg. If the instructions for your machine specify that the yeast is to be placed in the pan first, reverse the order in which you add the liquid and dry ingredients.

2 Sprinkle over the flour, ensuring that it completely covers the liquid. Add the salt, sugar and butter in three separate corners of the bread machine pan. Make a small indent in the centre of the flour (but not down as far as the liquid) and add the yeast.

3 Set the bread machine to the dough setting; use basic dough setting (if available). Press Start.

4 Lightly grease a 23cm/9in square cake tin (pan). When the dough cycle has finished, remove the dough from the machine and place it on a lightly floured surface.

5 Knock the dough back (punch it down) gently, then roll it out to form a square that is approximately 30cm/12in.

6 Brush the dough with the melted butter for the filling and sprinkle it with the sultanas, candied peel, currants, brown sugar and mixed spice, leaving a 1cm/½in border along one edge.

7 Starting at a covered edge, roll the dough up, Swiss (jelly) roll fashion. Press the edges together to seal. Cut the roll into 12 slices and then place these cut side uppermost in the prepared tin.

COOK'S TIP
Use icing (confectioners') sugar instead of caster sugar and make a thin glaze icing to brush over the freshly baked buns.

8 Cover the dough with oiled clear film (plastic wrap). Leave to rise in a warm place for 30–45 minutes, or until the dough slices have doubled in size. Meanwhile preheat the oven to 200°C/400°F/Gas 6.

9 Bake the buns for 15–20 minutes, or until they have risen well and are evenly golden all over.

10 Leave them to cool slightly in the tin before turning them out on to a wire rack to cool further.

11 Make the glaze. Mix the caster sugar with 60ml/4 tbsp water in a small pan. Heat gently, stirring occasionally, until the sugar is completely dissolved. Then increase the heat and boil the mixture rapidly for 1–2 minutes without stirring, until syrupy.

12 Stir the orange flower water into the glaze and brush the mixture over the warm buns. Serve slightly warm.

Per bun Energy 287kcal/1208kJ; Protein 6.1g; Carbohydrate 43.5g, of which sugars 16.6g; Fat 11.1g, of which saturates 2.3g; Cholesterol 26mg; Calcium 85mg; Fibre 1.3g; Sodium 243mg.

MARZIPAN AND ALMOND TWISTS

If you like almonds, you'll love these. Amaretto liqueur, marzipan and flaked almonds make up a triple whammy.

90ml/6 tbsp water
1 egg
60ml/4 tbsp Amaretto liqueur
350g/12oz/3 cups unbleached white bread flour
30ml/2 tbsp skimmed milk powder (non fat dry milk)
40g/1½oz/3 tbsp caster (superfine) sugar
2.5ml/½ tsp salt
50g/2oz/¼ cup butter, melted
7.5ml/1½ tsp easy bake (rapid-rise) dried yeast
115g/4oz/1 cup ground almonds
50g/2oz/½ cup icing (confectioners') sugar
2–3 drops of almond essence (extract)
1 egg, separated
10ml/2 tsp milk
flaked (sliced) almonds, for sprinkling

MAKES 9

1 Pour the water, egg and Amaretto into the bread machine pan. If the instructions for your machine specify that the yeast is to be placed in the pan first, reverse the order in which you add the liquid and dry ingredients.

2 Sprinkle over the flour, ensuring that it covers the liquid. Add the skimmed milk powder. Place the sugar, salt and butter in separate corners of the bread pan. Make a small indent in the centre of the flour (but not down as far as the liquid) and pour the easy bake dried yeast into the hollow.

3 Set the bread machine to the dough setting; use basic dough setting (if available). Press Start. Lightly grease two baking sheets and set aside.

4 Make the marzipan filling. Mix the ground almonds, icing sugar, almond essence, egg white and 15ml/3 tsp water in a bowl and set aside. In a separate bowl, beat the egg yolk with 10ml/2 tsp water.

5 When the dough cycle has finished, remove the dough from the machine and place it on a lightly floured surface. Knock it back (punch it down) gently and then roll it out into a 45 × 23cm/18 × 9in rectangle. Cut this in half lengthways to make two 23cm/9in squares.

6 Spread the filling over one of the squares to cover it completely. Brush some beaten egg yolk mixture over the remaining square and place it egg side down on top of the marzipan filling.

7 Cut nine strips, each 2.5cm/1in wide. Cut a lengthways slit near the end of one of the strips. Twist the strip, starting from the uncut end, then pass the end through the slit and seal the ends together, with egg mixture. Repeat with the remaining strips.

8 Place the twists on the baking sheets and cover with oiled clear film (plastic wrap). Leave in a warm place to rise for 30 minutes or until doubled in size.

9 Meanwhile, preheat the oven to 200°C/400°F/Gas 6. Mix the remaining egg yolk mixture with the milk and brush the mixture over the twists to glaze. Sprinkle with a few flaked almonds and bake for 12–15 minutes, or until golden. Turn out on to a wire rack to cool.

Per twist Energy 331kcal/1389kJ; Protein 8.2g; Carbohydrate 44.3g, of which sugars 14.4g; Fat 13.6g, of which saturates 4.1g; Cholesterol 56mg; Calcium 113mg; Fibre 2.2g; Sodium 68mg.

COCONUT MILK SUGAR BUNS

A hint of coconut flavours these spiral-shaped rolls. Serve them warm or cold with butter and preserves.

1 Pour the coconut milk, milk, egg and vanilla essence into the bread machine pan. If the instructions for your bread machine specify that the yeast is to be placed in the pan first, reverse the order in which you add the liquid and dry ingredients to the pan.

2 Sprinkle over the flour, then the coconut, ensuring that the liquid is completely covered. Add the salt, caster sugar and butter, placing them in separate corners of the bread pan. Make a small indent in the centre of the flour (but not down as far as the liquid) and add the yeast.

3 Set the bread machine to the dough setting; use basic dough setting (if available). Press Start. Then lightly oil two baking sheets.

4 When the dough cycle has finished, remove the dough and place it on a lightly floured surface. Knock it back (punch it down) gently. Divide the dough into 12 equal pieces and cover these with oiled clear film (plastic wrap).

5 Take one piece of dough, leaving the rest covered; roll it into a rope about 38cm/15in long.

115ml/4fl oz/½ cup canned coconut milk
115ml/4fl oz/½ cup milk
1 egg
2.5ml/½ tsp natural vanilla essence (extract)
450g/1lb/4 cups unbleached white bread flour
25g/1oz/⅓ cup desiccated (dry unsweetened shredded) coconut
2.5ml/½ tsp salt
50g/2oz/¼ cup caster (superfine) sugar
40g/1½oz/3 tbsp butter
5ml/1 tsp easy bake (rapid-rise) dried yeast
50g/2oz/¼ cup butter, melted
30ml/2 tbsp demerara (raw) sugar

MAKES 12

6 Curl the rope into a loose spiral on one of the prepared baking sheets. Tuck the end under to seal. Repeat with the remaining pieces of dough, spacing the spirals well apart.

7 Cover with oiled clear film and leave to rise in a warm place for 30 minutes, or until doubled in size. Preheat the oven to 220°C/425°F/Gas 7.

8 Brush the buns with the melted butter and sprinkle them with the demerara sugar. Bake for 12–15 minutes, or until the buns are golden. Turn out on to a wire rack to cool.

Per bun Energy 210kcal/887kJ; Protein 4.6g; Carbohydrate 37.2g, of which sugars 8.6g; Fat 5.8g, of which saturates 3.7g; Cholesterol 26mg; Calcium 74mg; Fibre 1.5g; Sodium 137mg.

APPLE AND SULTANA DANISH PASTRIES

These Danish pastries are filled with fruit and are beautifully light and flaky.

FOR THE DANISH PASTRY
1 egg
75ml/5 tbsp milk
225g/8oz/2 cups unbleached white
bread flour
15g/½oz/1 tbsp caster (superfine) sugar
2.5ml/½ tsp salt
140g/5oz/⅔ cup butter, softened
7.5ml/1½ tsp easy bake (rapid-rise)
dried yeast

FOR THE FILLING
25g/1oz/2 tbsp butter
350g/12oz cooking apples, diced
15ml/1 tbsp cornflour (cornstarch)
25g/1oz/2 tbsp caster (superfine) sugar
30ml/2 tbsp water
5ml/1 tsp lemon juice
25g/1oz/3 tbsp sultanas (golden raisins)

TO FINISH
1 egg, separated
flaked (sliced) almonds, for sprinkling

MAKES 12

1 Place the egg and milk in the bread pan. Reverse the order in which you add the liquid and dry ingredients if necessary. Sprinkle over the flour, covering the liquid. Add the sugar, salt and 25g/1oz/ 2 tbsp of the butter in separate corners.

2 Make a shallow indent in the centre of the flour; add the yeast. Set the bread machine to the dough setting; use basic dough setting (if available). Press Start. Lightly oil two baking sheets.

3 Shape the remaining butter into a block 2cm/¾in thick.When the dough cycle has finished, remove the prepared dough and place it on a lightly floured surface. Knock it back (punch it down) gently and then roll it out into a rectangle that is slightly wider than the butter block, and just over twice as long.

4 Place the butter on one half, fold the pastry over it, then seal the edges, using a rolling pin. Roll the butter-filled pastry into a rectangle 2cm/¾in thick, making it twice as long as it is wide. Fold the top third down and the bottom third up, seal the edges, wrap in clear film (plastic wrap) and chill for 15 minutes. Repeat the folding and rolling process twice, giving the pastry a quarter turn each time. Wrap in clear film; chill for 20 minutes.

5 Make the filling. Melt the butter in a pan. Toss the apples, cornflour and sugar in a bowl. Add to the pan and toss.

6 Add the water and lemon juice. Cook over a medium heat for 3–4 minutes, stirring. Stir in the sultanas.

7 Leave the filling to cool. Meanwhile, roll out the pastry into a rectangle measuring 40 × 30cm/16 × 12in. Cut into 10cm/4in squares. Divide the filling among the squares, spreading it over half of each piece of pastry so that when they are folded, they will make rectangles.

8 Brush the pastry edges on each square with the lightly beaten egg white, then fold the pastry over the filling to make a rectangle measuring 10 × 5cm/4 × 2in and press the edges together firmly. Make a few cuts along the long joined edge of each pastry.

9 Place the pastries on the baking sheets, cover them with oiled clear film (plastic wrap) and leave to rise for 30 minutes.

10 Preheat the oven to 200°C/400°F/ Gas 6. Mix the egg yolk with 15ml/1 tbsp water and brush over the pastries. Sprinkle with a few flaked almonds and bake for 15 minutes, or until golden. Transfer to a wire rack to cool.

APRICOT STARS

When in season these light pastries can be decorated with fresh apricots.

1 quantity Danish pastry – see Apple
and Sultana Danish Pastries

FOR THE FILLING
50g/2oz/½ cup ground almonds
50g/2oz/½ cup icing
(confectioners') sugar
1 egg, lightly beaten
12 drained canned apricot halves

FOR THE GLAZE
1 egg yolk
30ml/2 tbsp water
60ml/4 tbsp apricot jam

MAKES 12

1 Roll out the pastry into a rectangle measuring 40 × 30cm/16 × 12in. Cut into 10cm/4in squares. On each square, make a 2.5cm/1in diagonal cut from each corner towards the centre. Mix the ground almonds, icing sugar and egg together. Divide the filling among the pastry squares, placing it in the centre.

2 Beat the egg yolk for the glaze with half the water. On each square, fold one corner of each cut section to the centre. Secure with the glaze. Place an apricot half, round side up on top in the centre.

3 Lightly oil two baking sheets. Place the pastries on them and cover with oiled clear film (plastic wrap). Leave to rise for 30 minutes or until doubled in size. Preheat the oven to 200°C/400°F/Gas 6.

4 Brush the pastries with the remaining egg glaze and bake them for 15 minutes, until golden. While the stars are cooking, heat the apricot jam in a small pan with the remaining water. Transfer the cooked pastries on to a wire rack, brush them with the warm apricot glaze and leave to cool.

Per pastry Energy 208kcal/869kJ; Protein 2.7g; Carbohydrate 23.6g, of which sugars 8.1g; Fat 12.1g, of which saturates 7.7g; Cholesterol 48mg; Calcium 42mg; Fibre 1.1g; Sodium 116mg.
Per star Energy 220kcal/920kJ; Protein 4.1g; Carbohydrate 22.8g, of which sugars 8.4g; Fat 13.2g, of which saturates 6.9g; Cholesterol 59mg; Calcium 58mg; Fibre 1.1g; Sodium 105mg.

TEABREADS AND CAKES

Rich cakes filled with nuts, spices, dried fruits or chocolate are all part of this diverse range of breads. A bread machine is the perfect tool for mixing and rising the rich doughs of Continental specialities, often prepared for special occasions. It's also good for baking traditional teabreads which combine a light texture and a good flavour. Classic cakes, such as Coconut Cake and Gingerbread can easily be baked in a bread machine.

BANANA AND PECAN TEABREAD

This moist, light teabread is flavoured with banana, lightly spiced with nutmeg and studded with sultanas and pecan nuts. Weigh the bananas after peeling them – it is important to use the precise quantities given.

SMALL

75g/3oz/6 tbsp butter, softened
150g/5½oz/generous ¾ cup caster
(superfine) sugar
2 eggs, lightly beaten
175g/6oz/1½ cups self-raising
(self-rising) flour, sifted
150g/5½oz peeled ripe bananas
70ml/2½fl oz/5 tbsp buttermilk
1.5ml/¼ tsp baking powder
2.5ml/½ tsp freshly grated nutmeg
100g/3½oz/generous ½ cup sultanas
(golden raisins)
65g/2½oz/generous ½ cup pecan
nuts, chopped
15ml/1 tbsp banana or apricot
jam, melted
15ml/1 tbsp banana chips

MEDIUM

100g/3½oz/7 tbsp butter, softened
175g/6oz/⅞ cup caster sugar
2 large eggs, lightly beaten
200g/7oz/1¾ cups self-raising
flour, sifted
200g/7oz peeled ripe bananas
85ml/3fl oz/6 tbsp buttermilk
2.5ml/½ tsp baking powder
5ml/1 tsp freshly grated nutmeg
125g/4½oz/⅔ cup sultanas
75g/3oz/¾ cup pecan nuts, chopped
30ml/2 tbsp banana or apricot
jam, melted
30ml/2 tbsp banana chips

LARGE

115g/4oz/½ cup butter, softened
200g/7oz/1 cup caster sugar
3 eggs, lightly beaten
225g/8oz/2 cups self-raising
flour, sifted
200g/7oz peeled ripe bananas
100ml/3½fl oz/7 tbsp buttermilk
2.5ml/½ tsp baking powder
5ml/1 tsp freshly grated nutmeg
140g/5oz/scant 1 cup sultanas
75g/3oz/¾ cup pecan
nuts, chopped
30ml/2 tbsp banana or apricot
jam, melted
30ml/2 tbsp banana chips

MAKES 1 TEABREAD

1 Remove the kneading blade from the bread pan, if detachable. Line the base of the pan with baking parchment.

2 Cream the butter and caster sugar in a mixing bowl until pale and fluffy. Gradually beat in the eggs, beating well after each addition, and adding a little of the flour if the mixture starts to curdle.

3 Mash the bananas until completely smooth. Beat into the creamed mixture with the buttermilk.

4 Sift the remaining flour and the baking powder into the bowl. Add the nutmeg, sultanas and pecans; beat until smooth.

5 Spoon the mixture into the prepared pan and set the bread machine to the bake/bake only setting. Set the timer, if possible, for the recommended time. If not check the cake after the shortest recommended time. Bake the small or medium cake for 50–60 minutes, and the large cake for 65–70 minutes. Use the light crust setting if available.

6 Remove the pan from the bread machine. Leave it to stand for about 5 minutes, then turn the cake out on to a wire rack.

7 While the cake is still warm, brush the top with the melted jam and sprinkle over the banana chips. Leave to cool completely before serving.

Per cake Energy 3277kcal/13745kJ; Protein 52.8g; Carbohydrate 413.7g, of which sugars 239.9g; Fat 168.2g, of which saturates 69.2g; Cholesterol 1263mg; Calcium 1056mg; Fibre 13.1g; Sodium 1701mg.

PEANUT BUTTER TEABREAD

Peanut butter gives this teabread a distinctive flavour and interesting texture.

1 Remove the kneading blade from the bread machine pan, if it is detachable, then line the base of the pan with baking parchment.

2 Cream the peanut butter and sugar in a bowl together until light and fluffy, then gradually beat in the egg(s).

3 Add the milk and flour and mix with a wooden spoon.

COOK'S TIP
Leave a rough finish on the top of the cake before baking to add character.

SMALL
75g/3oz/⅓ cup crunchy peanut butter
65g/2½oz/⅓ cup caster
(superfine) sugar
1 egg, lightly beaten
105ml/7 tbsp milk
200g/7oz/1¾ cups self-raising
(self-rising) flour

MEDIUM
115g/4oz/⅓ cup crunchy
peanut butter
75g/3oz/scant ½ cup caster sugar
1 egg, lightly beaten
175ml/6fl oz/¾ cup milk
300g/10½oz/generous 2½ cups
self-raising flour

LARGE
195g/4¾oz/scant ½ cup crunchy
peanut butter
125g/4½oz/scant ¾ cup caster sugar
2 eggs, lightly beaten
200ml/7fl oz/⅞ cup milk
400g/14oz/3½ cups self-raising flour

MAKES 1 TEABREAD

4 Spoon the mixture into the prepared bread pan and set the machine to the bake/bake only setting.

5 Set the timer, if possible for the recommended time. If, on your bread machine, the minimum time on this setting is for longer than the time here, set the timer and check the cake after the shortest recommended time. Bake the small cake for 40–45 minutes, medium for 55–60 minutes and large for 60–65 minutes. Use the light bake setting if available.

6 The teabread should be well risen and just firm to the touch. Test by inserting a skewer in the centre of the teabread. It should come out clean. If necessary, bake for a few minutes more.

7 Remove the bread pan from the bread machine. Leave to stand for 5 minutes, then turn on to a wire rack to cool.

Per cake Energy 1527kcal/6439kJ; Protein 45.8g; Carbohydrate 238.4g, of which sugars 81.2g; Fat 48.8g, of which saturates 11.8g; Cholesterol 196mg; Calcium 497mg; Fibre 10.3g; Sodium 400mg.

SMALL
120ml/generous 4fl oz/½ cup natural
(plain) live yogurt
1 egg
200g/7oz/1¾ cups plain
(all-purpose) flour
10ml/2 tsp baking powder
2.5ml/½ tsp ground nutmeg
65g/2½oz/5 tbsp butter
35g/1¼oz/3 tbsp light muscovado
(brown) sugar
25g/1oz/2 tbsp caster (superfine) sugar
40g/1½oz/½ cup goji berries
40g/1½oz/¼ cup walnuts, chopped
50g/2oz/⅝ cup ready-to-eat dried
apricots, chopped

MEDIUM
200ml/7fl oz/⅞ cup natural
live yogurt
1 egg
280g/10oz/2½ cups plain flour
12.5ml/2½ tsp baking powder
4ml/⅘ tsp ground nutmeg
75g/3oz/6 tbsp butter, softened
45g/1¾oz/3 tbsp light muscovado sugar
30g/generous 1oz/2¼ tbsp caster sugar
50g/2oz/⅝ cup goji berries
50g/2oz/½ cup walnuts, chopped
75g/3oz/generous ½ cup ready-to-eat
dried apricots, chopped

LARGE
210ml/7½fl oz/scant 1 cup natural
live yogurt
2 eggs
350g/12½oz/3 cups plain flour
15ml/3 tsp baking powder
5ml/1 tsp ground nutmeg
85g/3oz/6tbsp butter, softened
45g/1¾oz/3 tbsp light muscovado sugar
45g/1¾oz/3 tbsp caster sugar
65g/2½oz/⅝ cup goji berries
65g/2½oz/generous ½ cup
walnuts, chopped
75g/3oz/generous ½ cup ready-to-eat
dried apricots, chopped

MAKES 1 TEABREAD

GOJI BERRY AND YOGURT TEABREAD

Packed full of fruit and nuts, this healthy teabread is equally delicious served as a mid-morning snack or a tea-time treat. Goji berries are vitamin-rich and are becoming more popular and widely available.

1 Mix the yogurt and egg(s) together and pour into the bread machine pan.

2 Sift the flour and baking powder together. Stir in the nutmeg. Add the butter and rub in with your fingers until the mixture resembles fine breadcrumbs. Stir in the sugars.

3 Mix in the goji berries, walnuts and apricots. Add to the bread machine pan.

4 Set the machine to the cake setting, light crust, 500g, if available. Remove the bread pan at the end of the cycle. Leave to stand for 5 minutes, then turn out the cake on to a wire rack to cool.

COOK'S TIP
If your machine does not have a cake setting, or if you prefer, you can mix the cake by hand, then bake it in the machine. Mix the yogurt and egg into the dry mixture. Stir in the nuts and fruits. Remove the kneading blade from the bread pan, line the pan with baking parchment and place the mixture in the pan. Cook on the bake setting for 45 minutes for small, 50 minutes for medium and 60–65 minutes for large, or until risen and firm to the touch. Test it is cooked by inserting a skewer into the centre: it should come out clean.

Per cake Energy 1928kcal/8097kJ; Protein 34.3g; Carbohydrate 274.4g, of which sugars 121.7g; Fat 84.8g, of which saturates 38.3g; Cholesterol 151mg; Calcium 642mg; Fibre 11.6g; Sodium 631mg.

STRAWBERRY TEABREAD

*Perfect for a summertime treat, this hazelnut-flavoured teabread
is laced with luscious fresh strawberries.*

SMALL
115g/4oz/1 cup strawberries
115g/4oz/½ cup butter, softened
115g/4oz/generous ½ cup caster
(superfine) sugar
2 eggs, beaten
140g/5oz/1¼ cups self-raising
(self-rising) flour, sifted
25g/1oz/¼ cup ground hazelnuts

MEDIUM
170g/6oz/1½ cups strawberries
140g/5oz/⅔ cup butter, softened
140g/5oz/¾ cup caster sugar
2 eggs, beaten
15ml/1 tbsp milk
155g/5½oz/1⅛ cups self-raising
flour, sifted
40g/1½oz/⅓ cup ground hazelnuts

LARGE
175g/6oz/1½ cups strawberries
150g/5½oz/⅔ cup butter, softened
150g/5½oz/¾ cup caster sugar
3 eggs, beaten
175g/6oz/1½ cups self-raising
flour, sifted
40g/1½oz/⅓ cup ground hazelnuts

MAKES 1 TEABREAD

1 Remove the kneading blade from the bread machine pan, if it is detachable, then line the base of the pan with baking parchment.

2 Hull the strawberries and chop them roughly. Set them aside. Cream the butter and sugar in a mixing bowl until pale and fluffy.

3 Gradually beat in the eggs and milk (if you are making the medium cake), beating well after each addition to combine quickly without curdling.

4 Mix the self-raising flour and the ground hazelnuts together and gradually fold into the creamed mixture, using a metal spoon.

5 Fold in the strawberries and spoon the mixture into the pan. Set the bread machine to the bake/bake only setting. Set the timer, if possible, for the recommended time. If, on your machine, the minimum time on this setting is for longer than the time suggested here, set the timer and check the cake after the shortest recommended time. Bake the small cake for 40–45 minutes, medium for 50–55 minutes and large for 55–60 minutes. Use the light bake setting if available.

6 Test by inserting a skewer in the centre of the teabread. It should come out clean. If necessary, bake for a few minutes more.

7 Remove the bread pan. Leave the teabread to stand for 5 minutes, then turn out on to a wire rack to cool.

Per cake Energy 2119kcal/8862kJ; Protein 31.3g; Carbohydrate 237.4g, of which sugars 130.2g; Fat 122.9g, of which saturates 66.7g; Cholesterol 645mg; Calcium 385mg; Fibre 7.2g; Sodium 1022mg.

RUM AND RAISIN LOAF

Juicy raisins, plumped up with dark rum, flavour this tea-time loaf.
Serve just as it is or lightly toasted, with butter.

SMALL

75g/3oz/generous ½ cup raisins
22ml/1½ tbsp dark rum
1 egg, lightly beaten
170ml/6fl oz/1⅔ cup + 1 tbsp milk
350g/12oz/3 cups unbleached white
bread flour
1.5ml/¼ tsp ground ginger
25g/1oz/2 tbsp caster (superfine) sugar
2.5ml/½ tsp salt
40g/1½oz/3 tbsp butter
5ml/1 tsp easy bake (rapid-rise)
dried yeast
10ml/2 tsp clear honey, warmed

MEDIUM

90g/3¼oz/⅔ cup raisins
30ml/2 tbsp dark rum
1 egg, lightly beaten
250ml/9fl oz/generous 1 cup milk
500g/1lb 2oz/4½ cups unbleached
white bread flour
2.5ml/½ tsp ground ginger
40g/1½oz/3 tbsp caster sugar
3.5ml/¾ tsp salt
50g/2oz/¼ cup butter
7.5ml/1½ tsp easy bake dried yeast
15ml/1 tbsp clear honey, warmed

LARGE

100g/3½oz/⅔ cup raisins
45ml/3 tbsp dark rum
1 egg, lightly beaten
320ml/11fl oz/1⅓ cups milk
600g/1lb 5oz/5¼ cups unbleached
white bread flour
5ml/1 tsp ground ginger
40g/1½oz/3 tbsp caster sugar
5ml/1 tsp salt
65g/2½oz/5 tbsp butter
7.5ml/1½ tsp easy bake dried yeast
15ml/1 tbsp clear honey, warmed

MAKES 1 LOAF

1 Place the raisins and rum in a small bowl and leave to soak for 2 hours. Drain any remaining liquid into the bread machine pan. Add the egg and milk. If necessary for your machine, reverse the order in which you add the liquid and dry ingredients.

2 Sprinkle over the flour, ensuring that it covers the liquid completely. Add the ground ginger. Add the caster sugar, salt and butter, placing them in separate corners of the bread machine pan. Make a small indent in the centre of the flour (but not down as far as the liquid) and pour in the dried yeast.

3 Set the bread machine to sweet/basic, with raisin setting if available, light crust. Size: 500g for small, large/750g for medium, or 1kg/2lb for large. Press Start. Add the raisins when the machine beeps during the kneading cycle.

4 Remove the bread at the end of the baking cycle and turn out on to a wire rack. Brush the top with honey and leave the loaf to cool.

Per loaf Energy 1939kcal/8198kJ; Protein 41.1g; Carbohydrate 357.7g, of which sugars 91g; Fat 43.1g, of which saturates 23.9g; Cholesterol 282mg; Calcium 573mg; Fibre 12.4g; Sodium 428mg.

RASPBERRY AND ALMOND TEABREAD

*Fresh raspberries and almonds combine perfectly to flavour this
mouthwatering cake. Toasted flaked almonds make a crunchy topping.*

1 Remove the kneading blade from the
bread machine pan, if it is detachable,
then line the base of the pan with
baking parchment.

2 Sift the self-raising flour into a large
bowl. Add the butter and rub in with
your fingertips until the mixture
resembles fine breadcrumbs.

3 Stir in the caster sugar and ground
almonds. Gradually beat in the egg(s).
If making the small or large teabread,
beat in the milk.

4 Fold in the raspberries, then spoon
the mixture into the prepared pan.
Sprinkle over the flaked almonds.

SMALL
140g/5oz/1¼ cups self-raising
(self-rising) flour
70g/2½oz/5 tbsp butter, cut into pieces
70g/2½oz/generous ⅓ cup caster
(superfine) sugar
25g/1oz/¼ cup ground almonds
1 large egg, lightly beaten
30ml/2 tbsp milk
115g/4oz/1 cup raspberries
22ml/1½ tbsp flaked (sliced) almonds

MEDIUM
175g/6oz/1½ cups self-raising flour
90g/3½oz/7 tbsp butter, cut into pieces
90g/3½oz/⅓ cup caster sugar
40g/1½oz/⅓ cup ground almonds
2 large eggs, lightly beaten
140g/5oz/1¼ cups raspberries
30ml/2 tbsp flaked almonds

LARGE
225g/8oz/2 cups self-raising flour
115g/4oz/½ cup butter, cut into pieces
115g/4oz/generous ½ cup caster sugar
50g/2oz/½ cup ground almonds
2 large eggs, lightly beaten
45ml/3 tbsp milk
175g/6oz/1½ cups raspberries
30ml/2 tbsp flaked almonds

MAKES 1 TEABREAD

5 Set the bread machine to the bake/
bake only setting. Set the timer, if
possible, for the recommended time.
If not, set the timer and check after
the shortest recommended time. Bake the
small loaf for 40–45 minutes, the medium
for 55–60 minutes and the large for
65–70 minutes or until well risen.
Use the light crust setting, if available.

6 Test by inserting a skewer into the
centre of the teabread. It should come
out clean.

7 Remove the pan from the machine.
Leave to stand for 5 minutes, then turn
out on to a wire rack to cool. This cake
is best eaten on the day it is made, when
the fresh raspberries will be at their best.

Per cake Energy 1722kcal/7212kJ; Protein 34.3g; Carbohydrate 192.5g, of which sugars 84.4g; Fat 96.1g, of which saturates 42.6g; Cholesterol 353mg; Calcium 469mg; Fibre 11.3g; Sodium 631mg.

SMALL
115g/4oz/⅔ cup pitted dates
grated rind and juice of ½ lemon
115g/4oz/1 cup self-raising
(self-rising) flour
2.5ml/½ tsp each ground cinnamon,
ginger and grated nutmeg
50g/2oz/¼ cup butter
50g/2oz/¼ cup light muscovado
(brown) sugar
15ml/1 tbsp treacle (molasses)
30ml/2 tbsp golden (light corn) syrup
40ml/2½ tbsp milk
1 egg
40g/1½oz/⅓ cup chopped walnuts

MEDIUM
140g/5oz/scant 1 cup pitted dates
grated rind and juice of 1 lemon
170g/6oz/1½ cups self-raising flour
3.5ml/¾ tsp each ground cinnamon,
ginger and grated nutmeg
75g/3oz/6 tbsp butter
75g/3oz/6 tbsp light muscovado sugar
22ml/1½ tbsp treacle
45ml/3 tbsp golden syrup
60ml/4 tbsp milk
1 large egg
50g/2oz/½ cup chopped walnuts

LARGE
155g/5½oz/scant 1 cup pitted dates
grated rind and juice of 1 lemon
200g/7oz/1¾ cups self-raising flour
5ml/1 tsp each ground cinnamon,
ginger and grated nutmeg
100g/3½oz/scant ½ cup butter
100g/3½oz/scant ½ cup light
muscovado sugar
22ml/1½ tbsp treacle
45ml/3 tbsp golden syrup
75ml/5 tbsp milk
1 large egg
65g/2½oz/generous ½ cup chopped walnuts

TOPPING FOR ALL SIZES OF LOAF
25g/1oz/2 tbsp butter
50g/2oz/¼ cup light muscovado sugar
22ml/1½ tbsp plain (all-purpose) flour
3.5ml/¾ tsp ground cinnamon
40g/1½oz/⅓ cup chopped walnuts
MAKES 1 CAKE

TREACLE, DATE AND WALNUT CAKE

Layered with date purée and finished with a crunchy sugar and walnut topping, this cake is absolutely irresistible.

1 Remove the kneading blade from the bread pan, if it is detachable. Line the base of the pan with baking parchment. Place the dates, lemon rind and juice in a saucepan, add 60ml/4 tbsp water and bring to the boil. Simmer until soft. Purée in a blender or food processor until smooth.

2 Sift the flour and spices together. Cream the butter and sugar until pale and fluffy. Warm the treacle, golden syrup and milk in a pan, until just melted then beat into the creamed butter mixture. Add the egg and beat in the flour mixture, then stir in the chopped walnuts.

COOK'S TIP
You could try decreasing the topping ingredients by 25 per cent if you are making a small cake.

3 Place half the mixture in the bread pan. Spread over the date purée, leaving a narrow border of cake mix all round. Top with the remaining cake mixture, spreading it evenly over the date purée.

4 Set the bread machine to the bake/bake only setting. Set the timer, if possible for the recommended time. If not, set the timer and check after the shortest recommended time. Bake the small cake for 30 minutes, medium for 40 minutes and large for 50 minutes. Use the light bake setting if available.

5 Mix the topping ingredients together, sprinkle over the nearly baked cake and cook for 15–20 minutes more, until the topping bubbles and the cake is cooked.

6 Remove the bread pan from the machine. Leave to stand for 15 minutes, then turn out on to a wire rack to cool.

Per cake Energy 1771kcal/7445kJ; Protein 29.7g; Carbohydrate 256.9g, of which sugars 169g; Fat 76.6g, of which saturates 31.4g; Cholesterol 457mg; Calcium 447mg; Fibre 9.6g; Sodium 573mg.

Hazelnut Twist Cake

Easy to make yet impressive, this sweet bread consists of layers of ground nuts, twisted through a rich dough, topped with a maple-flavoured icing.

230ml/8fl oz/1 cup water
1 egg
450g/1lb/4 cups unbleached white bread flour
45ml/3 tbsp skimmed milk powder (non fat dry milk)
grated rind of 1 orange
2.5ml/½ tsp salt
50g/2oz/¼ cup caster (superfine) sugar
75g/3oz/6 tbsp butter, melted
7.5ml/1½ tsp easy bake (rapid-rise) dried yeast
flaked (sliced) almonds or slivered hazelnuts, to decorate

For the Filling
115g/4oz/1 cup ground hazelnuts
100g/3½oz/1 cup ground almonds
100g/3½oz/scant ½ cup light muscovado (brown) sugar
2.5ml/½ tsp freshly grated nutmeg
2 egg whites
15ml/1 tbsp brandy

For the Topping
60ml/4 tbsp icing (confectioners') sugar
15ml/1 tbsp hot water
30ml/2 tbsp natural maple syrup

Serves 6–8

1 Pour the water and egg into the bread pan. Reverse the order in which you add the wet and dry ingredients if necessary. Sprinkle over the flour, covering the liquid. Add the milk powder and orange rind. Place the salt, sugar and butter in separate corners. Make a shallow indent in the centre of the flour; add the yeast.

2 Set the bread machine to the dough setting; use basic dough setting (if available). Press Start. Lightly oil a 23cm/9in springform ring cake tin (pan).

3 When the dough cycle has finished, place the dough on a lightly floured surface. Knock it back (punch it down) gently, then roll it out to a 65 × 45cm/ 26 × 18in rectangle. Cut the dough in half lengthways.

4 Make the filling by mixing all of the ingredients in a bowl. Divide the filling in half. Spread one portion over each piece of dough, leaving a 1cm/½in clear border along one long edge of each piece.

5 Starting from the other long edge, roll up each piece of dough, Swiss (jelly) roll fashion. Place the two pieces next to each other and twist them together.

6 Brush the ends of the dough rope with a little water. Loop the rope in the prepared springform tin and gently press the ends together to seal.

7 Cover the tin with lightly oiled clear film (plastic wrap) and then leave the dough in a warm place for 30–45 minutes, or until it has risen and is puffy. Preheat the oven to 200°C/400°F/Gas 6.

8 Bake for 30–35 minutes, or until golden and well risen. Leave to cool slightly, then turn out on to a wire rack.

9 Make the icing by mixing the icing sugar, hot water and maple syrup in a bowl. Drizzle over the warm cake. Sprinkle with a few flaked almonds or slivered hazelnuts and leave to cool completely before serving.

Per serving Energy 557kcal/2337kJ; Protein 12.3g; Carbohydrate 73.8g, of which sugars 30.3g; Fat 25.3g, of which saturates 6.7g; Cholesterol 46mg; Calcium 171mg; Fibre 3.6g; Sodium 233mg.

COCONUT CAKE

Desiccated coconut gives this simple, speedy cake a wonderful moist texture and delectable aroma.

SMALL
75g/3oz/6 tbsp butter or margarine, softened
115g/4oz/generous ½ cup caster (superfine) sugar
2 eggs, lightly beaten
115g/4oz/1⅓ cups desiccated (dry unsweetened shredded) coconut
85g/3oz/¾ cup self-raising (self-rising) flour
55ml/2fl oz/¼ cup sour cream
5ml/1 tsp grated lemon rind

MEDIUM
100g/3½oz/7 tbsp butter or margarine, softened
140g/5oz/¾ cup caster sugar
2 large eggs, lightly beaten
140g/5oz/1⅔ cups desiccated coconut
100g/3½oz/scant 1 cup self-raising flour
70ml/2½fl oz/scant ⅓ cup sour cream
7.5ml/1½ tsp grated lemon rind

LARGE
115g/4oz/½ cup butter or margarine, softened
150g/5½oz/⅔ cup caster sugar
3 eggs, lightly beaten
150g/5½oz/1⅞ cups desiccated coconut
115g/4oz/1 cup self-raising flour
85ml/3fl oz/⅜ cup sour cream
10ml/2 tsp grated lemon rind

MAKES 1 CAKE

1 Remove the kneading blade from the bread pan, if detachable. Line the base of the pan with baking parchment.

2 Cream the butter or margarine and sugar together until pale and fluffy, then add the eggs a little at a time, beating well after each addition.

3 Add the desiccated coconut, flour, sour cream and lemon rind. Gradually mix together, using a non-metallic spoon.

4 Spoon into the pan and set the machine to the bake/bake only setting. Set the timer, if possible, for the recommended time. If, on your bread machine, the minimum time on this setting is longer than suggested here, set the timer and check after the shortest recommended time. Bake the small or medium cake for 40–50 minutes; large for 55–60 minutes.

5 Test if the cake is cooked after the recommended time by inserting a skewer into the centre of it. It should come out clean. If necessary, bake the cake for a few minutes more.

6 Remove the bread pan from the machine. Leave the cake to stand for 5 minutes, then turn the cake out on to a wire rack to cool.

COOK'S TIP
This cake is delicious with a lemon syrup drizzled over the top once it is cooked. Heat 30ml/2 tbsp lemon juice with 100g/3½oz/scant ½ cup granulated sugar and 85ml/3fl oz/ 6 tbsp water in a small pan, stirring constantly until the sugar has dissolved. Bring to the boil, then simmer for 2–3 minutes before drizzling the syrup over the warm coconut cake.

Per cake Energy 2205kcal/9244kJ; Protein 30.4g; Carbohydrate 277.5g, of which sugars 220.5g; Fat 116.3g, of which saturates 82.4g; Cholesterol 611mg; Calcium 313mg; Fibre 16.2g; Sodium 506mg.

GINGERBREAD

This tea-time favourite can be baked easily in your bread machine. Store it in an airtight tin for a couple of days to allow the moist sticky texture to develop.

1 Remove the kneading blade from the bread pan, if it is detachable, then line the base of the pan with baking parchment. Sift the flour, ginger, baking powder, bicarbonate of soda and mixed spice together into a large bowl.

2 Melt the sugar, butter, syrup and treacle in a pan over a low heat.

3 Make a well in the centre of the dry ingredients and pour in the melted mixture. Add the milk, egg and stem ginger and mix thoroughly.

4 Pour the mixture into the bread pan and set the machine to the bake/bake only setting. Set the timer, if possible, for the recommended time. If, on your machine, the minimum time on this setting is for longer than suggested here, set the timer and check the loaf after the shortest recommended time. Bake the small loaf for 40–45 minutes, medium for 50–55 minutes and large for 60–65 minutes, or until well risen.

5 Remove the bread pan. Leave to stand for 5 minutes, then turn on to a wire rack.

SMALL
175g/6oz/1½ cups plain (all-purpose) flour
3.5ml/¾ tsp ground ginger
5ml/1 tsp baking powder
1.5ml/¼ tsp bicarbonate of soda (baking soda)
2.5ml/½ tsp mixed (apple pie) spice
75g/3oz/6 tbsp light muscovado (brown) sugar
50g/2oz/¼ cup butter, cut into pieces
75g/3oz/scant ⅓ cup golden (light corn) syrup
40g/1½oz black treacle (molasses)
105ml/7 tbsp milk
1 egg, lightly beaten
40g/1½oz/¼ cup drained preserved stem ginger, thinly sliced

MEDIUM
225g/8oz/2 cups plain flour
5ml/1 tsp ground ginger
7.5ml/1½ tsp baking powder
2.5ml/½ tsp bicarbonate of soda
2.5ml/½ tsp mixed spice
115g/4oz/½ cup light muscovado sugar
75g/3oz/6 tbsp butter, cut into pieces
100g/3½oz/generous ⅓ cup golden syrup
50g/2oz black treacle
150ml/5fl oz/⅔ cup milk
1 egg, lightly beaten
50g/2oz/⅓ cup drained preserved stem ginger, thinly sliced

LARGE
250g/9oz/2¼ cups plain flour
7.5ml/1½ tsp ground ginger
7.5ml/1½ tsp baking powder
3.5ml/¾ tsp bicarbonate of soda
3.5ml/¾ tsp mixed spice
115g/4oz/½ cup light muscovado sugar
100g/3½oz/scant ½ cup butter, cut into pieces
115g/4oz/scant ½ cup golden syrup
50g/2oz black treacle
175ml/6fl oz/¾ cup milk
1 egg, lightly beaten
50g/2oz/⅓ cup drained preserved stem ginger, thinly sliced

MAKES 1 LOAF

Per loaf Energy 1721kcal/7215kJ; Protein 14g; Carbohydrate 222g, of which sugars 221.4g; Fat 92.7g, of which saturates 57g; Cholesterol 401mg; Calcium 1154mg; Fibre 0g; Sodium 1048mg.

MOCHA PANETTONE

30ml/2 tbsp instant coffee powder
140ml/5fl oz/scant ⅔ cup milk
1 egg, plus 2 egg yolks
400g/14oz/3½ cups unbleached white bread flour
15ml/1 tbsp cocoa powder (unsweetened)
5ml/1 tsp ground cinnamon
2.5ml/½ tsp salt
75g/3oz/6 tbsp caster (superfine) sugar
75g/3oz/6 tbsp butter, softened
7.5ml/1½ tsp easy bake (rapid-rise) dried yeast
115g/4oz plain Continental chocolate, coarsely chopped
45ml/3 tbsp pine nuts, lightly toasted
melted butter, for glazing

SERVES 8–10

COOK'S TIP
The dough for this bread is quite rich and may require a longer rising time than that provided for by your bread machine. Check the dough at the end of the dough cycle. If it does not appear to have risen very much in the bread pan, leave the dough in the machine, with the machine switched off and the lid closed, for a further 30 minutes to allow it to rise to the required degree.

Panettone is the traditional Italian Christmas bread from Milan. This tall domed loaf is usually filled with dried fruits; for a change try this coffee-flavoured bread studded with chocolate and pine nuts.

2 Sift the flour and cocoa powder together. Sprinkle the mixture over the liquid, ensuring that it is completely covered. Add the ground cinnamon. Place the salt, sugar and butter in separate corners of the bread pan. Make a small indent in the centre of the flour (but not down as far as the liquid) and add the yeast.

3 Set the bread machine to the dough setting; use basic dough setting (if available). Press Start. Lightly oil a 15cm/6in deep cake tin (pan) or soufflé dish. Using a double sheet of baking parchment that is 7.5cm/3in wider than the depth of the tin or dish, line the container so that the excess paper creates a collar.

4 When the dough cycle has finished, remove the dough from the machine and place it on a lightly floured surface. Knock it back (punch it down) gently. Gently knead in the chocolate and pine nuts and shape the dough into a ball. Cover it with lightly oiled clear film (plastic wrap) and leave it to rest for 5 minutes.

1 In a small bowl, dissolve the coffee in 30ml/2 tbsp hot water. Pour the mixture into the bread machine pan and then add the milk, egg and egg yolks. If the instructions for your bread machine specify that the yeast is to be placed in the pan first, simply reverse the order in which you add the liquid and dry ingredients.

5 Shape the dough into a plump round loaf which has the same diameter as the cake tin or soufflé dish, and place in the base of the container. Cover with oiled clear film and leave the dough to rise in a slightly warm place for 45–60 minutes, or until the dough has almost reached the top of the greaseproof paper collar.

6 Meanwhile, preheat the oven to 200°C/400°F/Gas 6. Brush the top of the loaf with the melted butter and cut a deep cross in the top. Bake the bread for about 10 minutes.

7 Reduce the oven temperature to 180°C/350°F/Gas 4 and continue to bake the panettone for 30–35 minutes more, or until it is evenly golden all over and a metal skewer inserted in the centre comes out clean without any crumb sticking to it.

8 Leave the panettone in the tin or dish for 5–10 minutes, then turn out on to a wire rack and leave it until it is quite cold before slicing.

Per serving Energy 336kcal/1412kJ; Protein 6.7g; Carbohydrate 47.3g, of which sugars 16.5g; Fat 14.7g, of which saturates 6.8g; Cholesterol 57mg; Calcium 90mg; Fibre 1.8g; Sodium 76mg.

EASTER TEA RING

*This Easter tea ring is too good to serve just once a year. Bake it as
a family weekend treat whenever you feel self-indulgent.
Perfect for a mid-morning coffee break or for tea time.*

*90ml/6 tbsp milk
1 egg
225g/8oz/2 cups unbleached white
bread flour
2.5ml/½ tsp salt
25g/1oz/2 tbsp caster (superfine) sugar
25g/1oz/2 tbsp butter
5ml/1 tsp easy bake (rapid-rise)
dried yeast
50g/2oz/½ cup ready-to-eat
dried apricots
15g/½oz/1 tbsp butter
50g/2oz/¼ cup light muscovado
(brown) sugar
7.5ml/1½ tsp ground cinnamon
2.5ml/½ tsp allspice
50g/2oz/⅓ cup sultanas (golden raisins)
milk, for brushing*

*FOR THE DECORATION
45ml/3 tbsp icing (confectioners')
sugar
15–30ml/1–2 tbsp orange liqueur or
orange juice
pecan nuts and candied fruits*

SERVES 8–10

1 Pour the milk and egg into the bread
machine pan. If the instructions for your
bread machine specify that the yeast is
to be placed in the pan first, simply
reverse the order in which you add the
liquid and dry ingredients.

2 Sprinkle over the flour, ensuring that
it covers the liquid. Add the salt, sugar
and butter, placing them in separate
corners of the bread pan. Make a small
indent in the centre of the flour (but not
down as far as the liquid) and add the
easy bake dried yeast.

3 Set the bread machine to the dough
setting; use basic dough setting (if
available). Press Start. Then lightly oil
a baking sheet.

4 When the dough cycle has finished,
remove the dough from the bread pan.
Place it on a surface that has been
lightly floured. Knock the dough back
(punch it down) gently, then roll it out
into a 30 × 45cm/12 × 18in rectangle.

5 Chop the dried apricots into small
pieces. Melt the butter for the filling and
brush it over the dough. Then sprinkle
the dough with the muscovado sugar,
ground cinnamon, allspice, sultanas and
chopped apricots.

6 Starting from one long edge, roll up
the rectangle of dough, as when making
a Swiss (jelly) roll. Turn the dough so
that the seam is underneath.

7 Curl the dough into a circle, brush the
ends with a little milk and seal. Place on
the prepared baking sheet.

8 Using a pair of scissors, snip through
the circle at 4cm/1½in intervals, each
time cutting two-thirds of the way
through the dough. Twist the sections so
they start to fall sideways.

9 Cover the ring with lightly oiled clear
film (plastic wrap) and leave in a warm
place for about 30 minutes, or until the
dough is well risen and puffy.

10 Preheat the oven to 200°C/400°F/
Gas 6. Bake the ring for 20–25 minutes,
or until golden. Turn out on to a wire
rack to cool.

11 While the tea ring is still warm, make
the decoration by mixing together the
icing sugar and liqueur or orange juice.
Drizzle the mixture over the ring, then
arrange pecan nuts and candied fruit on
top. Cool completely before serving.

VARIATION
There is a vast range of dried fruits
available in the supermarkets.
Vary the sultanas and apricots;
try dried peaches, mango, melon,
cherries and raisins, to name a few.
Just make sure that the total quantity
stays the same as in the recipe.

Per serving Energy 244kcal/1028kJ; Protein 4.4g; Carbohydrate 38.6g, of which sugars 18.2g; Fat 9.1g, of which saturates 4.5g; Cholesterol 44mg; Calcium 87mg; Fibre 1.1g; Sodium 65mg.

INDEX

The publishers would like to thank the following companies who lent equipment and flours: Prima International, Panasonic, PIFCO, Hinari, Pulse Home Products Ltd, West Mill Foods Ltd, Dove Farm Foods Ltd, Magimix